KHRUSHCHEV

KHRUSHCHEV

by Burt Hirschfeld

Hawthorn Books, Inc.   Publishers   New York

KHRUSHCHEV

First Edition: 1968

All photos are from Sovfoto except page 141, Eastfoto; page 163, United Nations; pages 151 and 183, Wide World.

Designed by Gene Gordon

1695

Author's Note

In the Soviet Union the private lives of public figures are considered, according to Marxist doctrine, to be of little consequence, and so they are seldom emphasized. Biographical material in encyclopedias, histories and newspaper reports is altered as an individual advances in the Communist hierarchy or falls from grace, the "facts" being shaped to the prevalent political line. This makes it somewhat easier to predict the Russian future than to learn about the past.

So it was with Nikita Khrushchev, who at the apex of his career was the most powerful man in Russia. A biographer is permitted no opportunity to study personal papers, letters or memoirs, and there is no possibility of checking details of his early life, since no records are available. But information about Khrushchev's childhood and early manhood has come forth from some official Soviet sources and from Khrushchev's own pronouncements, for he often referred to his youth.

All this, however, is ripe for change, subject to the political requirements of the men currently ruling the Union of Soviet Socialist Republics.

B. H.

1

He came into the world on April 17, 1894, sickly and scrawny, inciting scant optimism for his chance of survival. His father, Sergei Nikanorovich Khrushchev, considered his new son with hard peasant realism. Clearly the boy was not equipped for the rigors of life in the village of Kalinovka, which was in the province of Kursk, on the Russian side of the Ukraine border. It would be better if the child died before he took a firm hold on the emotions of the family. But the infant stubbornly refused to succumb and he was given a name, Nikita Sergeyevich, son of Sergei. It was a name people would come to know.

That same year, Nicholas II was crowned Czar, continuing the Romanov Dynasty, and bringing it one step closer to its demise.

The one hundred million peasants of Imperial Russia were an illiterate, and for the most part, landless group. Many of them, like the family of Sergei Nikanorovich, lived in a mud hut, an *izba,* with only a thatched roof to protect them from the elements. Many of them, like the grandfather of Nikita Sergeyevich, had been serfs, the property of landlords who could sell or exchange them at will for a rifle or a dog.

But these were changing times; industry was taking hold in the land of the Czars. It was a fortunate man who could secure a police permit enabling him to work in the factories or on the railroads, though he received few rubles for his twelve hours labor. Those who owned their own land worked it quietly, without complaining about taxes or restrictions, aware that too many others were forced to scratch in the fields of the rich in order to keep their families alive. Some peasants, desperate to earn a little more money, sought work in the factories even though they lacked the necessary papers and risked severe punishment.

In some of the more remote provinces, the landlords still acted as if the serfs had never been freed, conducting their affairs with the same cruel justice as did their forebears. A peasant who neglected to work a prescribed number of days, without pay, on the landlord's estate was flogged, and some died under the whip.

Each autumn Sergei Nikanorovich left his wife and children and went to work as a carpenter in the coalfields of the Donets Valley, the Donbas. He hoped to earn money enough to pay off the mortgage of the two and one-half acres of land he owned. Sergei had a second ambition: to purchase a good horse for himself. He never was able to buy the horse.

This then was the life that the infant Nikita seemed destined to live. But events were taking place that would transform his future, and that of Russia itself and of the world. There were those who celebrated the coronation of Czar Nicholas by plotting his overthrow. Such a man was Vladimir Ilyich Lenin (his real surname was Ulyanov), who formed an organization dedicated to a theory of total revolution as developed by Karl Marx. It was called the League of Struggle for the Emancipation of the Working Class. Later this became the Social Democratic Party, formed by a secret congress. The League sought strength from the workers of the towns and the cities: the proletariat. In 1898, a rugged young man joined the Social Democrats. His name was Joseph Dzhugashvili, later to be called Stalin, the "Man of Steel."

Czar Nicholas, aware of the growing unrest in his country, took note of it with typical arrogance, announcing that his rule would be the one that ended all ". . . interference by the common people in government . . ." saying further that " . . .

senseless dreams of parliamentary democracy" would not be tolerated. His reign, he insisted, would be an absolute monarchy, and death would be preferable to the demonstrations of defiance to that principle. There were those in Russia who were anxious to accommodate him.

In 1903, the Social Democrats split into two wings: Lenin's Bolsheviks, who were political opportunists, and the Mensheviks, holding more closely to theoretical Marxism.

None of this was of immediate concern to Nikita Khrushchev. The puny infant had grown into a muscular, active and energetic boy with a talent for playing the recorder. During his boyhood, Nikita worked both as a watchman and a shepherd, but he showed no special enthusiasm for his responsibilities.

When he was seven he began attending confirmation class at the church located in the center of the village. Years later he referred with some pride to this experience.

"I used to go every Sunday to the priest's house," he said, "to learn how to be a good Christian. When we did well we got sweets and tea to take home. Once I got a prize for learning the four Gospels by heart and reciting them nonstop in Church."

He also attended the village school for about two years, long enough to learn to read and write, to do simple arithmetic, and to quote from the Holy Scriptures. By peasant standards, Nikita was not without learning.

In 1904, Russia went to war with Japan, a war that dragged on endlessly with no apparent purpose, devouring thousands of peasants as fodder for the cannon. There were protests, waves of strikes, and many crop burnings on the plains of Russia. If Czar Nicholas heard the voice of the people, he gave no sign.

On Sunday, January 22, 1905, large crowds gathered outside the churches of St. Petersburg (called Petrograd from 1914 to 1924 and now named Leningrad), then the capital city of Russia. Led by a priest, Father Gapon, 150,000 people, well-mannered and unarmed, marched to the Winter Palace to petition for better working and living conditions. They carried pictures of the Czar and ikons and sang hymns and anthems.

Their approach was noted and orders were issued to the Imperial Guard. Mounted soldiers appeared in the streets, trapping the protesters in the squares. Men, women and children were shot down. A thousand were killed and thousands more were trampled by the high-stepping chargers of the troopers. Thousands more were arrested and exiled to the wasteland of Siberia.

Still the people refused to be silenced. There were general strikes during the rest of the year and considerable looting and burning.

During this, the war with Japan continued, going badly for Russia. The Pacific fleet suffered a major defeat and the sailors of the Black Sea fleet mutinied. The economy was on the verge of collapse and the governmental structure was gripped by inertia. Russia was faced with imminent disaster. It was the Finance Minister, Count Witte, a sophisticated public servant, who prevailed upon the Czar to permit the formation of a parliament, the Duma.

"A constitution has been granted," cried Leon Trotsky, "but the autocracy remains!"

Others agreed and resolved to work harder for political reform. Lenin, then living abroad since it was no longer safe for him in Russia, began to create a blueprint for revolution. Resistance to the tyranny of the Romanovs was toughening.

Nikita Khrushchev too was becoming tougher. His days as a shepherd had taught him self-reliance, and he had grown strong, an expert wrestler able to triumph over all the other boys of the village. He had also become a skillful dancer, which made him popular with the girls and he developed a reputation as a flirt.

By the time he was fifteen, Nikita had developed that deep love for the land that so often prevailed among the Russian peasantry. Despite widespread poverty and the difficulties of daily life, there were many joys to be gleaned: there were the

A mud hut.

sights and sounds and scents of the farmlands, the fish to be caught in the clear streams, the icy winters and the long summer days and the feel of hot dirt under bare feet.

Nikita was filled with a zest for life, a growing energy. His squat frame had filled out with layers of muscle and he was aware of his strength. There was a wariness and a rough insolence about him; he developed the native shrewdness of his peasant forebears and an intensifying hunger to improve his status.

Finally stirred to action, in 1908 the Czar proclaimed that "peasants in search of useful labor" could move freely around, something hitherto denied them. When Sergei Nikanorovich learned that it was now legal to work in the mines, he decided to take his son along. But the authorities in the mine fields rejected Nikita. They perceived a lack of respect in the way he held himself and too bold a look in his eyes. They decided that he might well be one of those troublesome revolutionaries who found fault with conditions in the mines.

Sergei turned elsewhere. A friend of his was a mechanic in the village of Yuzovka and he agreed to accept the boy as an apprentice. Nikita proved an apt student. His fingers were adept and he learned quickly as they travelled from pit to pit repairing the ancient machinery, or fixing the cars or clocks of the mine officials. The stocky peasant boy learned more than a trade; he saw the different ways in which men lived and the different rewards they received. He perceived the great gap that existed between the skimpy existence of his father and the lives of the affluent managers of the mines, who owned huge, richly furnished homes and dined on exotic foods.

When he was eighteen, Nikita found work as a mechanic at the Bosse factory, which manufactured hauling gear for the mines. He became friendly with Pantelei Makhinya, a miner and an amateur poet who, though not a political person, was dissatisfied with the quality of life under the Czar. It was in Makhinya's hut that Nikita first heard about the *Communist Manifesto* of Karl Marx and first heard it read.

12

The factory itself was a hotbed of Bolshevik activity. Here, illegal pamphlets were distributed among the workers. Here, Nikita came in contact with Bolsheviks who tested his interest and trustworthiness. Here, he was enlisted to distribute the underground newspaper, *Pravda,* a dangerous pastime with the police always hunting for revolutionaries. Of this period of his life, Khrushchev would say years afterward:

"I worked at a factory owned by Germans, at coal pits owned by Frenchmen, at a chemical plant owned by Belgians. There I discovered something about capitalists. They are all alike, whatever their nationality. All they wanted from me was the most work for the least money that kept me alive . . . I was not born a Communist . . ."

Russia under the Romanovs was becoming increasingly abrasive. In April, 1912, at the English-owned goldfield on the Lena River in Siberia, a strike broke out. To put it down, the military was summoned, and some two hundred laborers were killed. As word of this outrage spread across the land, strikes erupted everywhere, including the Bosse works. Young Khrushchev's part in this was minimal; he acted as a messenger for the strike committee. But this brought him to the attention of the police and he was promptly fired. He was not out of work for long, however, finding a job at the French-owned mines in Rutchenkovo.

Two years later, World War I began. As a skilled worker, Khrushchev avoided conscription. He also found a wife and in 1916 she gave him a son, and later a daughter. That same year Lazar Kaganovich, an active Bolshevik, came to Yuzovka to head the revolutionary group. He was intelligent and tough, a fighter who had seen the inside of a number of prisons because of his efforts in organizing strikes. A persuasive speaker, he hoped to win converts to the Bolshevik cause. Years afterward, Khrushchev would become his protégé, then his colleague and ultimately his enemy. Nikita listened and learned, but always the practical man, he was not yet ready to become a member of the Party.

War was catastrophic for Russia. In the first year of fighting, the casualties numbered nearly four million men. Then in 1916, an offensive was launched across the Ukraine and Poland, breaking the Austro-Hungarian armies. Abruptly the tide turned and the advance was halted. Russian soldiers, peasants mostly, and fed up with the hardship and the killing, began to mutiny.

Things were hardly better behind the lines. The winter was severe and people in the villages and cities were short of food. Nevertheless, the armies held and there appeared to be no cause for alarm. On March 8, 1917, Czar Nicholas departed for his headquarters at Mogilev, and on that same day the Revolution began.

The women of Petrograd sparked it. The shops were empty, there was little to eat, their sons and husbands were at war and being killed, there was little hope. Groups formed to voice their protests, demanding food and an end to the fighting, and soon they were moving along the broad avenues.

"Dai khleb!" they cried. "Give us bread!"

Soon some workers and a few companies of soldiers joined them. But darkness came on, the marchers dispersed and quiet descended on the city.

The next day they were back in the streets, the women, the workers and now the students, wearing their little blue caps. It was a spontaneous, general strike. Cossacks, the Czar's feared cavalry, milled aimlessly about on the outskirts of the crowds, not daring to charge the angry people as had been done so often in the past.

On Sunday, March 11, the protesters gathered in greater numbers than before, marching out of the Vyborg worker's district and across the frozen Neva River into the heart of Petrograd. There were some roadblocks and horse patrols, but they offered no serious opposition. It was not until they came to the main street, the Nevsky Prospect, that the shooting began. When it was over, sixty people were dead.

On the following morning, after a night in which they argued and debated, the soldiers joined the revolt. Prisoners were freed, arms were provided and, with a minimum of bloodshed, the people took control of Petrograd. The rest of Russia joined the Revolution with even less violence. It had been a spontaneous occurrence with no real leadership. The politicians watched these events but took no part in them. Those who would subsequently play key roles in the nation were not even in Russia. Trotsky was in New York; Stalin, in Siberia; Lenin, in Switzerland, and Nikita Khrushchev was busy in the Ukraine.

The Czar, from Mogilev, commanded the Duma to disband itself. The order was rejected. With restless crowds surging through the city demanding action, a Temporary Committee of the Duma was established as the first government of the new Russia.

At once, there were rivals for control. Socialist Democrats, Bolsheviks and Socialist Revolutionaries combined to form an emergency committee of their own. Confusion spread. The Duma Committee was unable to govern, having no communication with those who had actually made the Revolution. It was Alexander Kerensky, an anti-Marxist Socialist Revolutionary who provided the needed link between the Duma and the Soviet Committee. A Provisional Government came into being and a week after the uprising began, Czar Nicholas II abdicated.

Eight months later, on November 7, Lenin's followers overthrew the Kerensky Government. It was more a *coup d'état* than a revolution. In January, 1918, Lenin dissolved the Constituent Assembly, the first democratic parliament Russia had ever had. The dictatorship of the proletariat had taken over and soon blood would flow as Lenin moved to solidify his position as Chairman of the Council of People's Commissars.

Watchfully assessing all that was happening, Nikita Khrushchev, now twenty-four years old, understood the cold realities of the time and acted accordingly. He became a Bolshevik.

2

Comrade Khrushchev's advanced education swung into high gear in the toughest of schools—revolution and civil war. Soon after becoming a Bolshevik or Communist Party member, he joined the Red Army to play an active role in the bloody happenings in the days that came next.

Russia, immediately after the Revolution, was a place of chaos and terror. Even as the war against Germany went on, millions of army deserters fled the front; uprisings, plots and counter-plots, revolts and counter-revolts broke out. There were the Red Government, the White Government, and bandit governments. Food was in short supply, and there was famine and illness. Every day, factories closed, and unemployment became widespread. At the same time, prices zoomed to unprecedented heights; foodstuffs and other goods were hoarded. Houses belonging to landlords were burned and there was increased looting. And always there were political firebrands shouting simplistic slogans to incite the passions of the people, to win converts, to summon the people to action.

"All land belongs to the peasants!"

"The factories belong to the workers."

"No more rank. No more privilege."

During all this, Nikita Sergeyevich Khrushchev was a *politrabotnik*, a political worker, in the Red Army. Those tiny peasant eyes were shrewdly observing and learning the lessons that the difficult times taught. He watched as a passionate minority

16

under the command of Comrade Lenin rose to power, overcoming all enemies by means of violence and terror and laying the foundation for the dictatorship of the Communist Party over the people. In a nation with a population of more than 175,-000,000 persons, the Communist Party could claim fewer than 50,000 members in March, 1917. But Nikita Khrushchev saw beyond mere numbers, assessing the future coldly and accurately and linking his destiny irrevocably to the Communist Party.

For the young peasant there were many lessons to learn. None was more important than to view with distrust all foreign countries, especially capitalistic countries which were anxious to exploit the workers and the peasants and to reverse the forward thrust of the Revolution.

Lenin and his Bolsheviks were determined to take Russia out of the war as soon as possible, and the Allies were no less determined to keep Moscow in the fight. Allied troops were ordered into Russia to lend strength to those committed to the war against Germany. This meant helping those White Russian leaders who sought to overthrow the Bolsheviks.

Others contributed to the chaos. The Social Revolutionaries, for example, were still a potent force. They backed peasant uprisings around the country, and even tried to seize Moscow itself. But the attempt failed.

In order to suppress this opposition, Lenin organized the Cheka (Extraordinary Commission to Combat the Counterrevolution), forerunner of subsequent Soviet secret police organizations, in 1917. It was announced that: "The All-Russia Cheka is absolutely independent in its activity and is invested with the power to carry out searches, arrests and executions." The lengths to which the Cheka—"the fist of the working classes"—would go was spelled out in its newspaper, *Red Terror:*

Do not search for incriminating evidence as to whether a person opposed the Soviet with arms or with words. Your first duty is to ask him what class he belongs to, what were his origins, education and occupation. It is these questions which should decide the fate of the accused. This is the meaning and essence of the Red Terror.

Workers and peasants, among others, were arrested, many never to be seen alive again, as the Red Terror spread across Russia in a cruel effort to impose political orthodoxy on the people. Under the guise of eliminating counter-revolutionists, it murdered ordinary citizens who seemed to stand in the way of those lusting after power. It also killed Czar Nicholas and his family.

Nevertheless, opposition to the Bolsheviks continued. Officers of the late Czar, anxious for revenge, formed a Volunteer Army and launched a general offensive in 1919, moving almost to Moscow. They killed anyone thought to be a Bolshevik. Whenever they conquered an area, landlords promptly resumed control of their property. Peasants who were captured were hanged or shot.

When the Reds triumphed, the process was reversed. Landlords and priests, officers and shopkeepers were drowned or shot or hanged. In Siberia, when Whites captured Reds they burned them in the fireboxes of railroad locomotives. Death gave birth to hatred throughout the country.

Many changes took place. The Ukraine became an independent nation, and so did Georgia. There were riots in Baku, and Armenia was laid waste by the Turkish Army. In Central Asia, the Tajiks, the Kazakhs, the Turkomans and the Uzbeks all rose up against their Russian masters. The Whites, suffering heavy casualties, advanced on Petrograd. But no matter who controlled the countryside or the city, terror reigned.

Finally in 1919, the Communists began to gain the upper hand. The country they won, however, was ruined. There was unemployment, a shortage of clothing and fuel, and sickness. A terrible famine swept across the land.

In 1920, the famine struck at Nikita Khrushchev. His young

wife died of starvation, leaving him with two small children. He allowed little of the grief he felt to show as he assumed the role of both father and mother, accepting the hardships of life even as he accepted its rewards. Years later he would say: "Life is a great school. It thrashes and bashes and teaches you."

Khrushchev's role in all this political turmoil and conflict was minimal. As secretary of his Party cell in his Red Guard regiment, he distributed leaflets in an effort to win converts to the Bolshevik cause. He stayed alert to those who might wish to subvert the Revolution and reported them to his superiors. Nothing he did brought him to the attention of the hierarchy and, though the Party needed thousands of workers, he was not chosen for advancement.

Failing to distinguish himself, he concentrated on learning all he could about the new order of things. He soon understood that the individual meant nothing when placed against the Party. Moreover, agreements, whether between nations or between people, were ephemeral and subject to change when change was in order. His faith in the Party deepened, and he dedicated himself to the new system and to total war against all its enemies.

In 1922, the Civil War ended with the Bolsheviks victorious. Finland, the Baltic States and Poland, all had survived as independent nations; Russia, though maimed and diseased, was securely under the domination of the Communists.

With the fighting over, Khrushchev returned to civilian life in Yuzovka, a changed man. No longer was he merely a worker. Now he was a member of the ruling class, a member of the Party and an assistant manager of one of the mines.

Life continued to be hard, however, and many of the mines were forced to close down. There was little money to be earned and food, when it was available, was very expensive.

Nikita Sergeyevich vowed to survive and to prevail. He travelled around, seeking food from the villagers in the neighboring farm country. This was called bag trading and it was a venture tinged with danger. In one village, Khrushchev found himself surrounded by peasants who made no effort to conceal their animosity, even as they eyed the "city stuff" he carried for trading.

"You are one of these Bolsheviks?" a muscular peasant demanded.

Khrushchev measured the man in his worn boots and rough homespun trousers. "I am a worker, my friend, come after food. I have with me some fine objects that my friends in the city have asked me to trade. Are you interested?"

The peasant muttered almost inaudibly. "First the Germans, then the Poles and then the White Generals. All killing and looting. Now we have the Communists. This new government gives us nothing but more killing, more suffering, more stealing."

Khrushchev smiled and his moon face glowed with understanding. He decided it would be best to make no mention of his Party membership. "I bring some good boots to trade and some eider down comforters and other items. Do you have any meat or flour or lard?" His heavy-boned face seemed without guile and a moment later he was doing a thriving business.

Khrushchev drew a sharp lesson from these bag trading expeditions; as dangerous as it was to be a Communist in the country districts, it was equally dangerous in the cities not to be. The Party had once been an open forum with criticism permitted—but no longer. It was swiftly moving toward total orthodoxy with dissenting opinions viewed as heresy. Some people dared to complain.

"There is no longer any room for conflicting opinions in the Party," some workers said. "The Party is no longer a political organization, one among many others. Instead, it stands alone and permits no challenge."

In his official position of cell secretary, Khrushchev felt impelled to defend the Party. "The times are hard," he protested, "and many things must be done to secure the Revolution."

"That you would speak so is to be expected. You do because you are one who has pushed himself forward. That changes nothing. The Party apparatus has become a military machine and acts accordingly."

Khrushchev's face hardened when he heard such remarks. "To speak that way marks you as disloyal," he said slowly, aware that he lacked the necessary information to respond effectively with good answers to the arguments of the other miners. Convinced that he had to improve himself, he began to study, to read and to think about everything that was happening around him.

The complaints grew louder, more pointed. "Three years of bloodshed," the workers cried in despair. "Three years of hunger. Where are we with your party? We have starvation, chaos, the Soviet Government fighting against our village and factory soviets which are supposed to be independent councils. The trains do not run, there is conscription, the factories are closed and too many men are without work. This is what your revolution has brought us."

Khrushchev fought back, bellowing his answers, the big fists pounding the air and his face becoming livid. "Fools! Do you think Trotsky and Lenin fight for the Czarists? The Whites? They fight for you, the workers. Would you blame them for the scourges of war? For the Poles and the Germans? Did they make the harvest bad?"

Such replies began to come easily to Khrushchev and often won arguments, or ended them temporarily. But in truth they changed nothing. Life in the Union of Soviet Socialist Republics was hard and grim and more trouble lay ahead. It erupted at the Kronstadt naval base where the sailors of the fleet rose up against the Communist Government, disillusioned and weary of the poor rations on which they were forced to subsist.

"Soviets without Communists!" they cried. "Give back the power to the soviets!"

Lenin, fearful that the revolt might be contagious, might indeed overthrow the still shaky Communist structure, acted. He ordered the rebellious sailors suppressed. It was March and he dispatched loyal Red Army troops across the thick ice of the Bay of Finland to put down the uprising. The sailors were crushed.

To Lenin, the Kronstadt affair was ". . . the flash which lit up reality better than anything else." He understood that there were many among the peasants and workers who distrusted the Communists as much as they had distrusted the Czar.

"We must bring the people to their senses," Lenin declared, and ordered appropriate steps taken. Free discussion within the Party was virtually ended and it was decided that trade unions would no longer represent the interests of the workers against the owner of all the factories—the Government. It soon became apparent to many people that the unions had in fact become an instrument for controlling the workers.

But Lenin and the Tenth Congress of the Communist Party came to recognize that a ". . . direct transition to purely Socialist forms, to purely Socialist distribution, was beyond our strength, and that, unless we proved to be able to retreat and confine ourselves to easier tasks, we would be threatened with disaster."

Life eased somewhat. Changes were made, and the New Economic Policy was introduced. It permitted private enterprise in small industry and trade. Official food requisitioning was ended, and foreign capitalists were invited to reopen their Russian businesses. Even as these reforms took place, political oppression grew more intense and demanding, as members of the Party tried to widen and strengthen their authority.

To Cell Secretary Khrushchev, this meant wielding increasing power as he travelled from mine to mine, constantly demanding that the workers produce more.

"Everything depends on coal," he reminded them. "How can the factories produce boots and shirts if they do not have coal?

Lenin speaking in Moscow on May 5, 1920.

All you demand you must get with your own hands. No manna from the sky is going to come down to you. So beat with your picks with all your might."

Though his efforts resulted in stepped-up production, Khrushchev was not satisfied. In 1923 he began attending school in order to improve himself and to further his career. At the Donets Mining Technical School he studied a variety of subjects—algebra, physics, chemistry, Russian literature and language and, of course, Marxist political economy. He attended frequent cell meetings, readings of the official newspaper, *Pravda,* and general discussion meetings, which were actually designed for criticism by the members of other members, as well as for self-criticism. All this was designed to transform people into dedicated and loyal Communists.

In one respect, Khrushchev, and others like him, was fortunate. Lacking formal education, he had little to unlearn as he absorbed the tenets of Marxism. He accepted the teachings of that dogma without question, ignorant as he was of any other system of thought and untouched by the facts of history, politics or economics, as people in other countries might view them. He accepted and memorized many of the statements of Comrade Lenin such as:

> The scientific concept, dictatorship, means neither more nor less than unlimited power resting directly on force, not limited by anything, not restrained by any laws or any absolute rules. *Nothing else but that.*

It was a concept that came to condition his thinking more and more with the passage of time.

Khrushchev worked hard to learn such lessons and his success was evident to his superiors. After only one year at school, he was elected Party Secretary. This made him the chief of all the cell secretaries, the Party watchdog in the school and superior to all the students and the teachers. From this eminence, he worked closely with the local Cheka.

Elsewhere in the Soviet Union, fate took a hand in the future of the country. Vladimir Ilyich Lenin was sick and dying and already a struggle for power was going on among his followers. Leon Trotsky, Lenin's closest associate and creator of the Red Army, allied with forty-six other Party officials, criticizing the Party apparatus and forcing a public discussion of differences. The opposition group was headed by Joseph Stalin, the Secretary General, who was called the "Man of Steel."

In summary of his position, Trotsky wrote:

All those ought to be removed from their Party positions who at the first voice of criticism, of objection, of protest are inclined to demand one's Party ticket . . . all should feel from top to bottom that nobody dares to terrorize the Party.

In direct opposition to Trotsky, and anxious to assume Party leadership, Stalin sought to make it appear that he was a sworn disciple of the great Lenin and a defender of the True Faith. He attempted to answer Trotsky by quoting from Lenin's statements and writings. So shrewdly did he do this that many Party members came to believe that Trotsky was a "deviationist" addicted to Western ideas and so a dangerous force in Russia.

In truth, Lenin had never looked upon Stalin as his successor, saying of him, ". . . Stalin is too rude . . . the comrades should find a way to remove him [as Secretary General] . . . and appoint another man . . . more patient, more loyal, more polite, and more attentive to the comrades, less capricious . . ."

On January 24, 1924, Lenin died and the entire nation went into mourning. But it was Joseph Stalin who wrote and delivered an Oath to Lenin, dedicating himself and all Commu-

nists to fulfilling Lenin's "commandments." In celebration of
Stalin's declaration, Yuzovka was renamed Stalino for six
months and Party Secretary Khrushchev made an impassioned
speech to the workers.

That same year, Nikita Sergeyevich met Nina Petrovna, a
political science teacher. They were later married. Years after,
commenting to reporters in Washington, D.C., Mrs. Khrushchev said of their courtship: "We met in the same city, but
I did not teach him anything and he did not teach me."

By now the struggle for power in the Soviet Union had
surfaced so that functionaries like Khrushchev could see and
understand what was happening, taking sides as the battle lines
were formed. Draped in ideological terms, the battle was between those, like Trotsky, who believed in "perpetual revolution" and saw the hope for a poor and backward Russia
dependent on the triumph of revolutions in other, more richly
endowed nations; and those who felt that Lenin's vision of a
general European revolution was illusory. These men decided
that a Russia surrounded by hostile countries would have to
raise herself first and strengthen her internal condition before
attempting to establish Socialism in foreign lands. This concept
came to be known as "Socialism in One Country," and it was
this theory that Stalin clung to in opposing Trotsky for control
of the USSR.

With all this occurring, Khrushchev had a more pressing
problem to be concerned about—his own future. He completed
his education in 1925 and now had to find a way to support
himself, his children, and Nina Petrovna, and to carve a meaningful role for himself in the New Russia. To the bullet-headed
peasant, now in his thirty-second year, there was only one
place to do that—the Communist Party. He had never been a
full-time member of the Party apparatus, but that was an over-
sight he meant to correct.

3

Before too much time elapsed, the seriousness, the ability to communicate with both the workers and the peasants and the dedication of Nikita Khrushchev was noticed and acted upon at higher echelons. K. V. Moyseenko, Party Secretary of the Yuzovka region and one of Joseph Stalin's supporters, decided that Khrushchev could be an asset and appointed him Party Secretary in the Marinka district of Stalino, his first truly political post.

As an *apparatchik,* a member of the governing apparatus, Khrushchev was overseer of some four hundred square miles of territory which, though primarily industrial, contained considerable farmland also. Here he was almost supreme, liable only to Moyseenko and to the GPU, as the Secret Police was now called.

Soon Khrushchev was demonstrating his predisposition for travel, in order to place himself close to the people. He displayed his ability to understand their problems while, at the same time, persuading them to act in a fashion consistent with Party policy. During the pleasant summer months, he crisscrossed the district in a light wagon, pausing in towns and villages and at isolated farm houses. His broad grin and plain manner indicated that he was little different from those people of the soil. Nor did he let the bitter winters stop him. He would don a *kozhukh,* a coat of coarse sheepskin, with the wool next to his body for greater warmth, and make his visits in a horse-drawn sledge.

There was an infinite number of important tasks to be done. Factories had to be reopened and run at full capacity. Mines had to be kept in operation. Men without jobs had to be put to work and the peasants had to be encouraged to put in more time in their fields so they could grow more food for the cities.

There were other problems. Ukrainian nationalists roamed the countryside looting, killing and destroying property. They had to be eliminated, and they were, usually by force. The *besprisorni,* the wild, orphaned children, moved around singly or in packs, the wasted human residue of the civil war and the great famine. Khrushchev was anxious to reclaim these miserable young people for the nation and, with this in mind, he began a hostel for them. Still others, he put to work in irrigation projects, in digging canals or on the railroads.

His sincerity and efficiency were recognized and, in 1925, he was named a delegate to the Fourteenth All-Union Party Congress. It was at this conclave that the power struggle within the Party broke into the open.

Stalin and his backers were committed to the suppression of Lenin's statement criticizing the "Man of Steel." They aimed to smother all free discussion of policies. Their tactics were blatantly crude, but effective. Any speaker who rose in opposition was loudly heckled and insulted, preventing the delegates from hearing him and forcing him to deal with irrelevant questions. Chief of the Ukraine delegation was Lazar Kaganovich, Khrushchev's patron and a very able heckler, as were Moyseenko and Nikita Sergeyevich.

The Congress, and the events which soon followed, were of particular interest to Khrushchev. He observed carefully as Joseph Stalin scored telling victories over his enemies, routing them by an overwhelming vote, a vote gained because of his wily behind-the-scenes manipulations, and the work of his effective organization. When it was all over, Stalin had set himself up as dictator over the Party.

Nor did he stop there. Maneuvering swiftly to perpetuate and solidify his victory, Stalin eliminated his opposition in the city of Leningrad and replaced them with his supporters. All this was done before his enemies at the Congress could make their way back to that city.

Khrushchev was impressed by Stalin's political sagacity and ruthlessness. These were lessons he never forgot. He returned to Marinka convinced that he knew the direction in which the Soviet Union would move, and where the source of power was lodged. He vowed to act accordingly.

Some men might have felt content, even smug, at this point in their careers. Not Khrushchev. There had been thirteen hundred delegates at the Congress, representing about one million Party members. Thus Nikita Sergeyevich, after a mere seven years in the Party, was one of the top thirteen hundred. He intended to climb higher.

He had studied Stalin's direct and comparatively untroubled rise to power, had seen strikers shot down by the police at a mine on the outskirts of his own district and had bullied and coerced his own workers when they became too obstreperous and too demanding.

"Order," he was fond of telling them, "means discipline, workers' discipline."

So it was inevitable that he voiced enthusiastic agreement for an article in *Pravda* in October, 1926, which terminated all hope of democracy within the Party. The article was headlined "Against Discussion!" and outlined a five-point program to this end:

. . . because it shakes the very foundations of the dictatorship of the proletariat, the unity of the Party, and its dominant position in the country; because it serves the cause of petty groups which hanker for political democracy.

That same month Khrushchev read also the Declaration of Submission to the Party—to Joseph Stalin, actually—signed by his defeated opponents: Trotsky, Kamenev, Zinoviev, Piatakov and Sokolnikov. All were subsequently murdered by orders of Stalin. Khrushchev knew who was master in Moscow.

His education took another step forward that same month at the First All-Ukrainian Party Conference in Kharkov. There, he heard Kaganovich heap ridicule and scorn on all those who claimed that democracy within the Party had been wiped out.

In a naked distortion of words, the Party hierarchy, as represented by Kaganovich, manipulated language to support their own ambitions, to mean what they wanted it to mean. Kaganovich insisted that all persons did not have equal rights to question the decisions of the majority, saying that democracy in the Party was ". . . a tool, a means of raising the political activity of the masses."

When he finished speaking, Kaganovich sat down and a member of the opposition rose to challenge his point of view. This was the signal for Khrushchev to take the floor to make his first recorded speech, a speech in support of Kaganovich, a speech that revealed much about him and about the depth of his ambition and boldness.

"We have just heard the speech of Comrade Golubenko of Odessa," he began. "It is entirely clear to me that Comrade Golubenko intentionally slandered the Party and that he lied about the situation in our Party organization . . ." If his listeners thought Khrushchev would be satisfied merely to counter Golubenko's remarks, they underestimated this stocky peasant. He aimed at larger targets and struck out daringly.

"In my opinion," he bellowed, "today's speech of the oppositionist Golubenko entirely confirms the unscrupulous and superficial nature of the declaration of our opposition. Our Party organizations demand from the opposition that they totally submit to the decisions of the Fourteenth Congress and the Central Committee of the All-Union Communist Party. I believe that the declaration written by the opposition is not a sincere declaration. Unless the opposition entirely recognizes the decisions of the Fourteenth Party Congress, there can be no question of collaborating with them. Should this not be the case, then we ought to demand from the highest Party organs

A group of bezprizornye or orphan children.

that they apply repressive measures against the incorrigible members of the opposition, regardless of their former merits and positions."

Since Joseph Stalin had already accepted the sincerity of the signers of the declaration of submission, Khrushchev was moving out ahead, insisting on the total surrender of those still loyal to Lenin and his policies and demanding that punitive measures be taken against them. To many of his listeners, Khrushchev must have sounded like more of a Stalinist than even Stalin himself. To some it must have seemed as if Khrushchev was scouting the ideological territory in advance of the master, breaking new ground. And there must have been some in that audience who saw the speech for what it was, an audacious effort on the part of the man from Yuzkova to lift himself past those who stood higher than he did in the Party.

Here Khrushchev showed two facets of personal style that would remain part of his makeup through the years: the ability to deliver an insulting verbal attack studded with unproven assertions which he made seem factual; and his willingness to take any calculated risk, if the promised rewards were great enough.

A year later, at the Tenth Ukrainian Party Congress, he once again revealed his boldness. While others sought to deliver a final defeat to the opposition, he submitted some original ideas about Party organization, saying: "As we carry on the struggle against the opposition, we should not overlook practical questions of Party construction . . . I propose that secretariats of the regional Party committees be created in important industrial areas and districts . . .

"At the same time, the creation of secretariats will make it possible to free the district Party committees from petty, less important questions and to concentrate their attention on basic questions.

"My second proposal deals with the necessity of changing

32

the intervals between the elections of the Party cell bureaus and the convocation of district conferences . . ."

There were few people who misunderstood what he was saying: he anticipated tighter Party control at the cost of local elections and wanted to eliminate further criticism of the leadership. In this, he reflected the thinking of Comrade Stalin.

With these two speeches, Khrushchev showed himself to be a strict adherent of authoritarianism. Caught up in the grip of his own ambition, he had attached himself closely to Kaganovich, and so to Stalin. There were no doubts about right and wrong. He knew exactly where he was going.

His next promotion took him to Stalino and to near calamity. A scandal broke out in that region, and the leadership was accused of moral laxity, systematic drinking bouts, bribery, promiscuity, bad management, waste and excessive use of oppression. A purge was instituted and Khrushchev was transferred to Kiev. This was actually another promotion for him since Kiev was a much more interesting and important city than Stalino. Once again, he had demonstrated his growing ability to protect himself and to further his career, no matter what befell those around him.

During this time a conflict between Stalin and Nikolai Ivanovich Bukharin broke out. Bukharin was a brilliant but politically unreliable Party intellectual, the editor-in-chief of *Pravda,* who continued to agitate for a more liberal regime. With his typical brashness, Khrushchev injected himself into the squabble. In April, 1929, he said:

. . . there are some leading comrades who, admitting by word of mouth the correctness of those decisions, sabotage the work of the Central Committee and do not carry out assignments given by the Party. They want to cover up their deviation from the Leninist line by various slanders about oppression . . . But one should not deceive oneself by unanimous decisions. Some comrades, under the influence of difficulties, begin to waver . . .

Obviously Khrushchev was referring to Bukharin and his followers, an identification not made public until later in the year. Bukharin took the position that the daily needs of the people should not be sacrificed for the ambitions of the men heading the New Russia. He said they were so intent on making the Soviet Union into a world power, with a suitable military establishment, that they emphasized heavy industry at the expense of consumer goods and services.

In order to create and maintain heavy industry, a tax was placed on the peasants, and this was explained by Comrade Stalin: "This is an additional tax levied on the peasants for the sake of promoting industry, which works for the whole country, the peasants included."

And later, he added: "There are some people who do not like this [tax]. These comrades apparently fear the truth . . ."

Bukharin responded quickly, labelling this so-called tribute a ". . . military-feudal exploitation of the peasantry."

Angered by this opposition, Stalin struck back hard, but avoided a head-on confrontation, aware that he might be defeated. Very carefully, he prepared the ground for his eventual victory. Within the Politburo (Political Bureau), Stalin appeared to give in to his enemies and to compromise for the sake of Party unity.

Molotov, his close ally, remarked of this tactic: "When the fruit does not fall from the tree when you shake it, it means that the fruit is not yet ripe. Stalin can wait."

He waited and worked. From his eminence as Secretary General of the Party, Stalin was able to dismiss certain supporters of Bukharin from their jobs in the Party, replacing them with his own choices. Meanwhile his propagandists kept churning out their anti-Bukharin messages, calling for an intensification of the struggle against those labelled as Right Deviationists.

Bukharin was familiar with this strategy, saying: ". . . For several weeks I have not been on speaking terms with Stalin. He is an unscrupulous intriguer and subordinates everything to his desire to retain power for himself. In order to eliminate somebody . . . he changes theories . . . Now he has begun to retreat in order to finish us off . . ."

That year, 1929, with the struggle for internal supremacy continuing, Stalin wanted his strongest supporters close at hand. With this in mind, he summoned Kaganovich to Moscow to act as Secretary of the Central Committee of the All-Union Party. Not long afterward Khrushchev followed his mentor. The two men worked harmoniously in the years that followed—until the time came for Khrushchev to destroy Kaganovich.

4

To Khrushchev, then thirty-five years old, Moscow was a dream city in September, 1929. This was the hub of the Soviet Union, of Communism; the fountainhead of all power in Russia. It was the place where an ambitious man could advance himself, display his talents and win the rewards available for those who attained status in the apparatus.

For its inhabitants, however, Moscow was a living nightmare. Though large, it looked like a provincial city that had overflowed its boundaries. There was a dark and brooding quality about it and everywhere there was evidence of decay. No new buildings had been erected since 1904, nor new roads built, nor improvements of any kind made, and the scars of the 1905 revolution were still visible. Building walls were peeled and cracked, roofs leaked and roads were rutted and potted.

People lived where they could, crowded into basements and small rooms, two or three families living in one place frequently, grateful to be protected from the elements. Heat and light were generally in short supply, there was never enough food and there was no soap.

Yet there was a growing vitality in the city, an urgency to get things done and to look ahead to better times. People were hungry to learn so as to arm themselves for the future. They attended academies and technical institutes which were housed in the ancient mansions and palaces that had once belonged to the rich and the titled.

Writers and artists, inspired by the promise of the Revolu-

36

tion, worked, dreamed and talked about what lay ahead and about the benefits that would come to the Russian people. Ordinary workers were themselves gripped by this same optimistic fervor and viewed their futures as being locked in the sprockets, gears and drive shafts of the new machinery that everyone talked about. This machinery would produce all the marvelous items to make life better and more fruitful.

All this Khrushchev, Nina Petrovna, and his two children by his first marriage saw and understood. Though the housing shortage was severe, this was only a minor problem for Khrushchev and he soon had his family settled in quarters that were comfortable if not lavish. This was a good thing, too, for soon Nina Petrovna would bless him with another child, Rada.

Now Nikita Sergeyevich was able to direct his attention to his career. He enrolled in the All-Union Industrial Academy, one of only one hundred freshmen, and promptly discovered that he had landed in the midst of an internal conflict that threatened to consume the entire country, a struggle that was to display all the despotism of Stalin and the insensitive destructiveness of Stalinism.

It began in the summer of that year. Stalin attempted to collectivize the countryside and the activities of the people, especially to place agriculture under government control, to impose restrictions on what was planted and to inflict quotas on the farmers.

The reasoning behind this was simple: the Soviet Union was close to another famine and it was imperative that two million tons of grain be obtained in order to forestall it. Lacking the grain, people in the cities and towns would starve and the new industries would fail. Also threatened was the power of Joseph Stalin.

When the harvest was ready, the collectivization process was applied to the gathering of the grain in all its impersonal competence, displaying a ruthlessness such as the world had seldom ever seen. Years later Stalin would confide to England's Prime Minister, Winston Churchill, that this had been a more crucial period for Russia than the worst of World War II.

Perhaps. But for the peasants it was a time of total oppression that seemed to signal the end of their freedom and the confiscation of the product of their labors. They resisted and in so doing insured their own downfall. Mandates were issued in Moscow and carried out by local officials with cruel dispatch. Farmers were driven off their property, or liquidated; and where resistance was too firm, entire villages were deported to concentration camps.

"The Revolution is betrayed!" peasant leaders cried. "It is no different than life under the Czars. Fight back with every weapon at hand."

Enraged and bitter at what was happening to them, the peasants fought back in the only way they knew. Crops were burned, livestock slaughtered and tools broken. Stretches of rich farmland went unseeded and unworked. Inevitably, a great blight descended over the plains and cities of the New Russia. Soviet agriculture was ruined and decades would pass before it was able again to attain the productivity of 1929.

Stalin observed all this with a cold and cynical eye. "The Revolution," he said, "demands victims; even if the achievement of full-scale socialization of the countryside should demand twenty million peasant lives, we would not hesitate."

Under the circumstances, it was not strange that many ordinary people and Party members became critical of Stalin's policies and wanted to change them, and the leadership of the country as well. Party members began to openly question what was happening, but they soon found themselves under attack, accused of "Right Deviationism." Those in official quarters who failed to denounce the dissenters, even if they supported the supposed infallibility of Stalin and his colleagues, were labelled as ". . . conciliators towards the Right Deviationists."

Waves of doubt and despair broke out among the politically-minded students in Moscow's institutes of learning, and an increasing amount of criticism was levelled at the official line. Nowhere were the voices louder and the dissent more incisive, than at the Industrial Academy attended by Nikita Khrushchev.

That fall, at about the same time Khrushchev arrived in Moscow, the Party cell at the Academy had been purged of a number of militants who were, *Pravda* insisted, ". . . closely connected with the Bukharin group of young professors . . ." concluding that they had ". . . connived with the Rightists and shown an obviously conciliatory attitude toward them." This done, the cell bureau was dissolved and a new one "elected."

Despite this punitive action, opposition to the Government continued to mount in Moscow, especially in the Party cell at the Academy. For Khrushchev, this was a particularly difficult time. He was surrounded by bright-eyed young men and women, chosen to be the leaders of a new elite. Many of them, like himself, enjoyed talking and were quick to debate some obscure ideological question or expand on a fine political point, seeming to take pleasure in arguing for its own sake.

Khrushchev was no conversationalist, no dabbler in abstractions. Instead, he was addicted to attacking those with whom he disagreed, uttering long, declamatory monologues, shouting down objections, wheedling or bullying as was necessary to gain his ends. Against quick and cunning students, these techniques didn't always work, and he learned to watch, listen and wait for the right opportunity to speak—or even better, to act.

There was one member of the cell who especially troubled and puzzled Khrushchev. She was a thirty-two-year-old beauty named Nadezhda Alliluyeva, one of the most gifted of the students. A tense woman with sad, sensitive eyes, she gave evidence of a mounting disaffection with the policies of the ruling circles and displayed a growing anxiety for the future of Russia if changes were not made. Nadezhda Alliluyeva was the wife of Joseph Stalin.

Here was a situation that caused Khrushchev many hours of

troublesome thought. Were he to act in a manner demanded by the Party, he would expose the Right Deviationists in the cell, and so expose Stalin's wife. Would this be viewed as an indication of loyalty and dependability, or would it serve only to enrage the "Man of Steel"? And if he remained silent— would that be seen in a favorable light or as a failure to fulfill one's duty to the Party? It was a delicate problem and failure to solve it properly could mean the ruination of his career, even before it was well begun.

Meanwhile, the Bukharinites in the cell became bolder and elected eight of their supporters to represent the school at the upcoming Moscow Party conference. They began to voice their doubts more openly and in stronger language.

"All that is wrong is the doing of Comrade Stalin," one of their number stated angrily. "All power resides in his hands."

There was general agreement. "Collectivization is wrong and brutal and must be ended. What is required is a kind of organized capitalism."

"The Central Committee is at fault," another said. "It fails to lead. It lags behind."

Disturbed and confused by what he heard, Khrushchev cast anxiously about for some profitable means of solving his dilemma. To offend Joseph Stalin was a risk he dared not take, yet he felt it was imperative that he make clear to his superiors exactly where he stood in this struggle. The solution to his problem came in a single word. Kaganovich.

His old patron had achieved a lofty eminence and could make sure Khrushchev's loyalty became known to the top men in the Kremlin. At the same time he could go on record as fulfilling his responsibilities by reporting what he knew about the dissenters in the Academy cell, including Nadezhda Alliluyeva, protecting himself against the inevitable day of reckoning.

It was a well-designed move. In June, *Pravda* attacked conditions at the Academy, pointing out that not ". . . a single

Moscow's Red Square in 1929.

dissenting voice" had been raised against critics of the regime. Khrushchev had made no public statement on his position, but had protected himself, nevertheless. *Pravda* went further, hitting out at A. P. Shirin, Party Secretary of the Bauman District, which included the Academy, criticizing him for not interfering when some students demanded ". . . that another meeting be held that would revoke the elected delegates . . ."

Suddenly concerned by what was happening, Shirin convened the Party cell again, keeping it in session for two days during which it ". . . admitted its errors . . ." and rejected the eight delegates elected six days before.

A resolution was passed by the cell, one clause of which was aimed at unmasking those Rightists still unrevealed. It read:

In view of the fact that, within the cell of the Industrial Academy, a factional group of Rightists and an organized group of conciliators leaning towards the Rightists have existed for a long time, the Party cell considers it impossible that some comrades remain in the Academy, since after their graduation these comrades would be in no position to ensure the carrying of the general line of the Party. The bureau is assigned to carry out this decision in the shortest time, bringing up the question before the Central Committee.

To those who heard the clause read, two facts became clear: One, mention of the Central Committee meant that Stalin himself had been a close observer of what was going on at the Academy; two, any official of the Academy cell would now have direct access to the highest forum of the Communist Party, the Central Committee.

The newly elected cell secretary took note of this. His name: Nikita Sergeyevich Khrushchev.

Authorized now to denounce traitors within the Academy cell, Khrushchev went about his job with enthusiasm, unburdened by other responsibilities, and not at all concerned about his studies. How well he succeeded—especially in the delicate matter of Nadezhda Alliluyeva—was recognized at higher echelons and six months later he replaced A. P. Shirin as Secretary of the Bauman District.

A few weeks later Khrushchev received another political reward. He was elected to the City Party Committee, a group of fifteen persons under the authority of Lazar Kaganovich, himself a member of the Politburo as well as Secretary of the Central Committee. Kaganovich was a very important person to have for a friend. During the summer of 1931 Khrushchev was made Secretary of Moscow's Red Presnaya District, keeping control of the Bauman District at the same time. Only six months later he was appointed Second Secretary of the Moscow City Committee, directly under Kaganovich.

It was in the Red Presnaya District that Khrushchev gave another display of his drive and initiative. He created a system of "days" and "ten-day" periods, concentrating labor and equipment to speedily and forcefully achieve one goal or another. In this fashion he was able to expedite economic plans, particularly in the last quarter of the year when results of all projects were minutely appraised. These innovations were introduced subsequently into all Party organizations in the Moscow area.

For Khrushchev in those days, life was comparatively simple. His goals were those of the Party, held without question or doubt, and to fulfill them he utilized any method that worked. There was the progressive and premium piecework system, for example, an incentive system under which the basic pay for each unit of work increased progressively as a worker exceeded his quota. This heightened competition among the workers and gave a great advantage to the strong, who grew stronger as they earned more and were able to buy more food and eat better; the weak found their strength diminishing and their ability to work fell off accordingly.

Khrushchev had no interest in the human condition, except as it reflected on his ability to fulfill his quotas. He concentrated on percentages of production, on costs and results, on doing his part to achieve the current Five Year Plan.

"Raw materials matter," he liked to say. "And machines. These are the important things."

As for the men and women who fell aside, unable to meet arbitrary standards of production, they were easily replaced from the huge Russian population.

For Khrushchev, life now was altered radically. He moved in the rarefied atmosphere of Communist Party circles and found it important to consider not only his career but his very life and the well-being of his family each time he spoke or acted. A wrong word might confine a man to political oblivion and a serious error could cost him his life.

To the Party, it was proper to be dedicated, even fanatical. But not too dedicated, not too fanatical. Intelligence was important, but it was risky to display it blatantly. Steadiness of purpose and action were desirable, as was the ability to remain inconspicuous, to offer no threat to one's superiors. Faceless men echoing the Party line, speaking in the orthodox cadences of *Pravda,* sounding like Stalin himself, were most readily accepted. Khrushchev tried to become such a man.

He was not alone. Others were advancing through the Soviet ranks. They were strong, ambitious and dedicated men, grasping at the reins of power and learning how to use them. These men would be heard of later; some would live long and well, and others would meet shadowed and abrupt ends. There was Kaganovich. And Ordzhonikidze, close to Stalin, was killed one day, probably on the orders of the same Stalin. Voroshilov was the head of the Red Army. Lavrenti Beria served in the Caucasus but had valuable service in the Secret Police behind him. Anastas Mikoyan was in charge of all foreign trade; Bulganin: Chairman of the Moscow City Soviet. Georgy Malenkov worked in the Central Committee. Nikolai Yezhov was

44

looked upon by many as a Stalin man. Henry Yagoda managed the infamous labor camps. Sergei Kirov was boss of the city of Leningrad. And there were others, all tough men, shrewd, daring, seemingly cut of a single mold in their knee-boots and cloth caps, their shirts buttoned to the neck and their eyes focused on some distant goal. They were Khrushchev's colleagues, his friends and his competitors. He watched them closely, studying them, cataloguing their weaknesses for future reference.

These days Khrushchev was able to provide a pleasant life for Nina Petrovna and the children. They had a good apartment, a motorcar and no concerns about food or clothing. That was the advantage of being an *apparatchik*. There were also drawbacks. As a member of the apparatus, home and family took second place to Party loyalty and demands. That Khrushchev had recognized this fact of his life and made his peace with it became clear during the Slutsky affair.

The man Slutsky had written an article for the historical journal of the Communist Party, *Proletarian Revolution,* commenting on errors he believed Lenin had made. This drew the wrath of Joseph Stalin who wrote a letter to the editors taking them to task for printing Slutsky's article. He insisted that there was a need to ". . . raise the questions concerning the history of Bolshevism to the proper level, to put the study of the history of our Party on scientific, Bolshevik lines, and concentrate attention against the Trotskyites and all other falsifiers of the history of our Party by systematically ripping off their masks."

Stalin's intentions were obvious to those who wished to understand: to glorify his past exploits and elevate himself to the same exalted level as Lenin. This meant that history in Russia was to be revised, and Stalin's biography altered to suit his ambitions. The facts were to be rewritten as required.

Khrushchev got the message. He discovered that Slutsky

actually lived in the Red Presnaya District, and before much time passed the local Party unit expressed its resolve that Slutsky's article was a ". . . deliberate utilization of Party literature for propaganda of Trotskyism, the spearhead of the counterrevolutionary bourgeoisie." Not satisfied with this, Khrushchev began to maneuver until he was able to get Slutsky ejected from the Party, the near-ultimate punishment. In so doing he fortified his own position, and his actions were duly noted and favorably commented upon in a Red Party newspaper.

In 1932 the worst famine Russia had ever known spread across the land bringing with it a growing terror of Stalinism. Photographs of the "Man of Steel" and statues to his personal glory were seen everywhere. Yet, these seemed to have a reverse effect upon the people, and hatred for him mounted in both private and official circles. But few people could find the courage to stand up to him.

One who did was his wife, Nadezhda Alliluyeva. The daughter of an old revolutionary, she was an idealistic Communist and patriot. Anger and torment at what was happening had been building inside her for a long time, and finally, at a party given by Voroshilov, the melancholy young beauty spoke out. She charged that injustices were being committed against the Russian people and condemned the terror used against them. Food shortages had to be alleviated, she insisted, and she lamented the tragedy that had enveloped her country.

Stalin, always the crude and boorish man Lenin had distrusted, lashed out at her fiercely, rebuking her brutally. Distraught and near to tears, she fled the party. Stalin let her go, remaining to discuss political policy with his followers. When he returned home that night, it was to discover Nadezhda Alliluyeva in bed, a blanket pulled over herself, dead of a self-inflicted gunshot wound in the heart.

Her death altered nothing. Conditions in the Soviet Union worsened steadily, and the Party faithful were not to be troubled by the death of a single woman, whatever her name or point of view. But Stalin, concerned about the rising tide of criticism and fearful of how this might affect the country and himself, moved to obtain a reaffirmation of support from his colleagues. He went before the Politburo.

"Perhaps it is indeed true that I have become an obstacle in the unity of the Party," he said, and offered to resign. It was a device used, before and since, by demagogues and dictators, who were certain that such a dramatic gesture would excite public support while presenting a minimum of risk, since few people would dare call for such a move. So it was within the Politburo, which already was purged of its Right Wing members.

When Stalin finished speaking, there was a long, uncomfortable silence. Then Molotov was on his feet, saying it for them all. "Stop it!" he cried. "Enough! You know you have the Party's confidence . . ."

To that, Nikita Khrushchev would have heartily agreed. He had become one of Stalin's men and would remain so, until it suited him to ravage the "Man of Steel."

5

There was no end to what had to be done. Even as a new political system and a new economy were being imposed, as stumbling efforts to improve life for the people were being made, the cities had to be rebuilt. As secretary of the Moscow City Party Committee, Nikita Sergeyevich Khrushchev was confronted with many of the problems which existed in the capital city and was responsible for solving them. He attacked each with a steely directness and a commanding bluntness that inevitably got things done.

"At the construction sites," he said in the autumn of 1933, "as everywhere, mere words are not enough. We need a Bolshevist organized system, clearness of purpose, knowledge of the matter and ability to fulfill without fail the plan by the Party and Government."

His emphasis of the Party as a source of strength, wisdom and correctness of decision was not mere lip service. More and more he had come to understand that the Party was indeed the root of the power of the men who ruled in Russia and the device by which they continued themselves in power. For ultimate efficiency, he decided all control must reside in the Party, for all things stemmed from it—all right thinking and all reward.

Believing this, Khrushchev found it logical and easy to insist that the people who worked under him produce more. He levelled criticisms at construction bosses for the way in which they operated, demanding that they obtain more and better work from their labor gangs, and called for a tougher approach in order to achieve this.

"The success of construction," he declared, "depends on the workers' fulfillment of the norm. If you are chief of a construction site, encourage the better worker, help him, let him earn more, but at the same time carry on a decisive struggle against the self-seeker and the 'runner' who comes to the construction site to snatch wages and run away."

Convinced of the infallibility of Party wisdom and authority, and aware that failure was unacceptable to his superiors, he would accept no excuse for failure by those under him, demanding that all quotas be met, all questions answered and all problems solved. Under increasing pressures, the workers found it almost impossible to meet the demands made, and it was suggested to Khrushchev that local quotas be decreased. His response was typical:

"These harmful, disorganizing aspirations should be met with a severe rebuff. It is necessary to fight in a Bolshevist way so that every bricklayer, plasterer, and painter fulfills his norm of output. All kinds of opportunistic whisperers who attempt to revise the norms should be repulsed with all resoluteness . . ."

With an attitude so completely in keeping with Party thinking, it was inevitable that Khrushchev's talents be directed toward areas of greater responsibility. None was more important than the new project recently launched in the capital city— the Moscow subway.

Few people doubted that there were problems of greater urgency in the city—housing, jobs, roads, surface transportation, food and more—but the subway took priority, born out of the Communist need to celebrate its supremacy. This was going to be major evidence of that supremacy—the finest, most beautiful subway anywhere in the world. It would be a showplace to which visitors from abroad could come and of which they would speak when they returned to their homes, causing them to disseminate the message of the New Russia—that the Socialist way of life was superior to all others.

The subway, it was decided, would be built in record time.

Once begun, nothing was allowed to obstruct or to slow the work. Although the construction organization, *Metrostroi,* actually did the job, the project was too important for the engineers and construction foremen to be left in charge. All decisions, minor and major, including those of a highly technical nature, were passed on by the Moscow Party Committee, under the authority of Lazar Kaganovich and his energetic protégé, Comrade Khrushchev.

Here was an assignment that appealed to Khrushchev. Results were all that mattered; swift results. Boldness was important, boldness which involved disregarding the limitations of human flesh or the niceties of life. Many things were required: sacrifice, recklessness and a deep commitment that transcended the lack of advance information, experience or planning. That Nikita Khrushchev could act in such a fashion was his immediate strength and would carry him far; eventually these same qualities would cause his undoing. But that was later, much later.

No concern for human life was exhibited during the building of the subway—how many actually died has never been learned—and a self-serving date was selected for the completion of the first section, November 7, 1934, the seventeenth anniversary of the October Revolution.

Even official records concerned with the project revealed an elemental disregard for the welfare of the workers. Confessed G. Lomov, chief engineer: "When we constructed the subway we were, of course, aware of the fact that we were digging under an enormous city, that every disturbance of the foundations might lead to a disaster, but, nevertheless, during the first period of construction, we did not show particular vigilance."

This cautious statement does not admit that almost no safety measures were employed for fear that they might slow up construction. Once in a while the potential hazards were so apparent that the engineers hesitated, considering precautionary activity. When that happened Comrade Khrushchev inevitably appeared, his round face grave under a cloth cap and his little eyes darting around, demanding to know what was wrong and issuing orders for the work to continue.

In the seventh subway sector, because of the speed demanded of the laborers, no attempt had been made along the excavation route to shore up the buildings that perched along the sides of the deepening ditch. For a time it seemed that there was no concern for alarm, until a desperate cry went up.

"The house on the corner! It is beginning to fall!"

Frightened faces turned upward to perceive the terrifying truth. The loosened soil beneath the foundation was shifting, and the building could be seen to be moving. Word was passed to the inhabitants, and they were swiftly evacuated and work was stopped.

"The building foundation must be strengthened," workers assured each other.

The engineers, huddled together worriedly, appeared to agree and no effort was made to resume the work. At that moment, Khrushchev arrived, bullet-head bowed and a scowl wrinkling his brow at the sight of the idle men and equipment. He took in the situation at a single glance.

"What's the matter with you?" he challenged Chief Engineer A. M. Stepanov. "Are you afraid of buildings?"

Stepanov was unused to having his courage questioned but he ignored the pointed gibe. Instead he tried to make Khrushchev understand the problem, explaining that he and his associates agreed that the possibility of a disaster was great.

"Still," he went on, "if I am ordered to do so, I will proceed with the excavation without shoring up the buildings along the line."

Khrushchev absorbed this information silently, studying his

muddied boots while measuring the possible price in men and equipment against the need for speed. When he spoke at last, he supported the engineer's concern for the safety of his men and for the people living along the route. But he also made clear that, in his view, the work should resume and advance as swiftly as possible, because the project was worth the risk. Stepanov knew what was expected of him. Later he recalled: "Nikita Sergeyevich's words definitely persuaded us to go ahead with the work along the entire line."

There were occasions when caution was indicated. It was Kaganovich who made this point, appearing in the excavation one day and addressing the construction chief. "You are about to tunnel under a house which is full of Americans. For political considerations this house must not be permitted to fall down." Steps were taken and the house in question remained undisturbed, its occupants unaware of the special consideration they had received, consideration seldom provided for the homes of ordinary Muscovites.

Despite the accumulation of pressure, it began to appear that the first section of the subway would not be completed on schedule. Khrushchev was seen more frequently at the construction sites, his manner harsh and unrelenting.

"Comrade Kuzmin," he said pointedly to one engineer, "you promised to clear away the scaffolding by the twelfth of the month and let the assemblers begin working. But it seems that you deceived the Moscow Party Committee. Today is the tenth, and see for yourself what it looks like around here."

Kuzmin had little choice but to defer to Khrushchev. "Nikita Sergeyevich, we promised, and our crews will keep the promise."

This thinly veiled threat by Khrushchev served its purpose. Inspired by his words, and anxious not to displease the Moscow Party Committee in any way, engineers, technicians, foremen and laborers all remained on the job for forty-eight consecutive hours, straining to clear their sections of timber and scaffolding

The Moscow subway being built.

before the deadline. Woman-engineer Leonova worked five straight shifts, for example. All this dedication achieved its purpose. When, on the twelfth, Khrushchev returned, it was to view an uncluttered entrance hall in the station. He let it be known that he was pleased and hoped never to be disappointed.

But in another sector the work went badly, and Khrushchev again addressed the workers, ending his speech with an undisguised threat: "May I tell Lazar Moiseyevich (Kaganovich) that the station will be finished according to schedule?"

Concerned lest they incur Kaganovich's attention and wrath, the crews assured Khrushchev that the work would be done on time, and it was. Later the chief of that site gave appropriate credit: "We achieved this victory because the work . . . was directly guided and organized . . . by Nikita Sergeyevich Khrushchev."

The subway was pushed ahead with a kind of desperate urgency. Two tunnelling shields—one English made, the other a Russian copy—were used. These were circular steel and cast-iron rings which moved forward in the excavation in order to support the ground in advance of the tunnel lining. Each shield was able to advance at a prescribed speed every twenty-four hours while observing minimum safety conditions.

To Khrushchev, all this caution and slowness was unacceptable. He insisted that the tempo of operations be increased no matter how great the risks. He was obeyed despite the fact that no one knew with any degree of certainty what soil conditions were. As a result, a succession of deadly accidents occurred, which were described later in a Soviet publication:

The shield approached the silt—a brown fluid mass. The caisson (a watertight chamber which operated under increased air pressure) worked under an air pressure of 2.3 atmospheres. With every hour the conditions became more difficult. Sometimes the silt resisted and unprecedented efforts were necessary to top it, to save the tunnel, the machines, and, chiefly, the people. Once a fire broke out in the caisson. In order to avoid rapid spreading of the fire in compressed air rich in oxygen it became necessary to lower the air pressure, but this opened the way for the silt that poured in torrents into the shaft . . .

No report was made of how many lives were lost in this catastrophe, and the many others like it. Lives meant very little when the Party wanted to make a display of Socialist efficiency. As the projected completion date, November 7, came closer, added pressure was exerted to get the first section finished. No one was more active in bullying, wheedling and haranguing the workers than Comrade Khrushchev, issuing inspirational slogans which in fact were commands, stimulating the men to greater efforts and allowing the engineers no time to plan or to take even the most rudimentary safety measures. A witness wrote of these activities:

> Comrade Khrushchev constantly kept his eye on our work; every day the surveyor marked on a chart in Khrushchev's office the movement of our shields. At the slightest slowing down Khrushchev would immediately call in Comrade Tyagnibeda or Suvorov and demand an explanation as to why the slowdown had taken place and what the difficulties were. This constant vigilance of Comrade Khrushchev always inspired the workers to work even better.

Totally committed to the project, the Soviets turned to slave labor in building certain sections of the subway. Many of these men were dedicated Communists who had come to Russia seeking asylum from persecution in their own countries. One such was Valentin Gonzalez, known as "El Campesino," a hero of the Spanish Civil War. Toppled from his lofty status, he was forced to labor in the subway in order to rehabilitate himself. Of the experience he wrote:

The Russians are extremely proud of the Moscow underground. It is their prize exhibit for foreign delegations, journalists, and tourists. They claim it as a masterpiece of construction, and they are quite right. Only they forget to explain that it is a monument not only to Soviet engineering but also to the slave labor that went into its construction.

Almost ninety per cent of the construction workers were in a position similar to mine. Many of them were old fighters, former military leaders, or even NKVD (as the Secret Police were now called) men. They had fallen into disgrace and had been allotted this sort of work, which offered them the faint—the very faint—hope that their efforts would in time restore them to their former position in the ruling class . . . the alternative to this work was Siberia, and so they did all they could to follow the faint ray of hope.

In time, thanks to the labor of unnamed thousands of men and women and at the cost of uncounted sums of money and lives, the subway was completed. Decorated incongruously with all the glitter and indulgence of a Czar, it may very well have been the world's most beautiful underground railway. An official publication described it this way:

Over 70,000 square meters of marble were required for the stations of the first and second sections alone. This is one and a half times what was used in all the palaces of Czarist Russia during the fifty years preceding the Great October Socialist Revolution. Labradorite, an exceedingly beautiful and durable stone of a dark gray color, with sparkling ultramarine, went to decorate the columns and walls of several stations. Lavish use was made of porphyry, granite, bronze, smalto, and ceramic, as well as glazed panels. Many of the interiors were adorned with gold leaf, statuary, bas-reliefs and mosaics.

The first section of the subway cost about five hundred million rubles. Contrast this with the investment in consumer goods during the four years of the first Five Year Plan—an average of three hundred *million* rubles per year. During 1934, when the first section was finished, all gleaming brilliance and Socialist glory, the Soviet Union was able to produce an average of only one shoe for each of its people.

Yet that same year there were indications that life in Russia would soon become easier and more rewarding for the ordinary citizen. The second Five Year Plan was in operation and appeared to be functioning well, and there was the implicit promise of increased stability, a more leisurely rhythm.

Elsewhere in the world, events also appeared to be moving in favor of a Socialist system. Dictatorships had come to power in many European nations, Fascist governments that cried out for territorial aggrandizement and preached hatred. The United States, despite the efforts of its new President, Franklin Delano Roosevelt, was caught up in a deep and seemingly insoluble depression that threatened total ruination to the nation. England, that imperialistic bastion, was fiscally immobilized, without the strength or the will to act affirmatively. Thus, to many people in countries around the world, hope lay in the New Russia, a nation reborn where a great sense of purpose was apparent, a collective vitality that would allow nothing to deter it from bettering the lot of its people.

Or so it seemed. Few outsiders knew of the famine in the Ukraine, or of the thousands upon thousands of peasants murdered, dispatched to Siberia, exiled to salt mines and labor camps or sent to work and die in remote forestry preserves or government-owned coal mines. As to the rumored shortages in Russia of food, clothing, modern machinery—these, it was claimed, were only minor inconveniences soon to be alleviated.

One man who made no criticism of anything happening inside the USSR was Nikita Khrushchev. He was elected to the

57

Central Committee in 1934, a rising light in the Communist Party. His future was bright and reasonably assured.

But Joseph Stalin possessed no such optimism. Wherever he looked he saw enemies, threats to the nation and to himself, and he meant to end them and to fortify his hold on Russia. His weapons: terror, blood, murder.

The Great Purge was about to begin.

6

In 1934 Joseph Stalin became
convinced that Moscow was a den of his political enemies.
There were such men as Grigori Zinoviev and Leon Kamenev
returned from Siberia. Nikolai Ivanovich Bukharin was firmly
entrenched on the editorial board of the Great Soviet Encyclopedia. Other old Bolsheviks, many of them supporters of Trotsky, and opposed to Stalin personally or politically, although
no longer prominent in Party business, were still alive and therefore a threat to him and to his regime.

More worrisome still was the new generation of Communists,
young men, shrewd and perceptive, who were able to think for
themselves, to question and doubt. Such men loathed the tyranny
unloosed upon Russia and were scornful of those of Stalin's
former political opponents who had capitulated to his policies
in order to protect themselves. From Stalin's lofty but exposed
position, it must have seemed simple enough to purge the dissi-
dents from the Party and to banish many of them to the labor
camps for "re-education" under the watchful eye of Henry
Yagoda, the new police chief.

Convinced of the danger that existed in any opposition, Stalin
vowed to crush it. At the same time he displayed uncertainty
as to how this was to be done. He began by abolishing the GPU
as an independent department and shifted its duties to the People's Commissariat for Internal Affairs, the notorious NKVD;
the Attorney General was provided with authority to oversee
the NKVD; members of Stalin's former opposition were invited to join in creating a new constitution. To some, such

moves must have appeared like much needed reforms. Stalin soon disabused them of that idea, issuing wild and often cruel decrees. One held the entire family responsible for an act of treason committed by any one of its members, and it was demanded that children inform on their parents, and husbands on their wives. Not to do so meant severe punishment.

The primary issue dividing members of the apparatus seemed to be "reconciliation," the reconciliation of the old Bolsheviks with the then current official thinking. The possibility that any of the old revolutionaries were willing to submit was undoubtedly due to weariness and to the faint hope that, by outlasting the present terror, they would at least survive, and perhaps eventually triumph. The issue was argued in the streets and restaurants, in political meeting rooms, in the Politburo itself—had the time come to soften the rule by force and consolidate all groups, all segments of political thought?

Reconciliation was a threat to many Communists who opposed it with all their energy and authority. Others viewed it as a good thing, the salvation of the country, the binding up of ancient political wounds for the benefit of the Soviet Union and all its people.

Sergei Kirov, head of the Party in Leningrad and a member of the Politburo, was foremost among the proponents of reconciliation. He was a short, handsome man. His pale gray eyes were far-seeing and chilly, revealing nothing of his highly developed intelligence or the hard edge of his character. A skilled orator, he had developed a fine grasp of the popular mood, and could manipulate his listeners to do his bidding. Dedicated to the success of the Revolution, he could be cruel in his methods of attaining it, though he was not vengeful. Now he claimed that the time had come for the leaders of Russia to accept their former enemies back into the fold for the sake of harmony and progress.

Since Kirov dared to stand openly against the barbaric practices of the NKVD, he appeared to many as the protector of the ordinary man. With his reputation growing, he was greeted with extensive applause at the Congress of the Victors in February, 1934, applause no less than that accorded to Stalin himself. Kirov was soon made a Secretary of the Central Committee, solidifying his hold on the reins of power. Then in November, at a plenary session of the Central Committee in Moscow, which was designed to speed the reconciliation, he dominated the meeting.

His mounting influence and real strength was noted, without approval, in high places and it became inevitable that efforts must be made to stop his advance. Once set in motion, events moved with dramatic impact.

On December 1, at 4:30 in the afternoon, Kirov was working in his Leningrad office when he was interrupted. A young man, Leonid Nikolayev, had somehow penetrated the security screen established around Kirov and had gained entry to his private office. He drew a pistol from under his coat and, with cool efficiency, killed Kirov.

The main witness to the murder was a man named Borisov. The next day he was in an automobile accident in which all the passengers escaped unharmed except Borisov. He was killed.

As for Nikolayev, he was hurriedly tried, judged guilty and executed, as were 15 young Communists known to be associated with him. It was publicly announced that Borisov was a Fascist agent in the service of a foreign power. Extending the dimensions of the murder plot, the authorities turned their attention to 104 other people, all of whom had been in prison long before Kirov was killed. They were shot.

Abruptly, and with no announced explanation, the tale about Nikolayev being a Fascist was put aside. Now the murder of Kirov was blamed on the followers of Zinoviev and Kamenev. Claims were made that Leningrad, as well as other localities, was infested with oppositionists, and steps were taken against them. Ten thousand people were summarily taken into custody and sent by train to the dreaded labor camps.

61

Zinoviev and Kamenev were charged with being responsible for Kirov's death and sentenced to prison. That wasn't enough for Joseph Stalin. He wanted confessions that could be made public and that would permit him to characterize the two men with the odious label of Trotskyite. (Leon Trotsky was then in exile spreading the truth about Stalin's Russia, a symbol of all opposition and a very real danger to the "Man of Steel.")

The day after Kirov's murder, Stalin arrived in Leningrad accompanied by Molotov, Voroshilov and Nikita Khrushchev, among others, who were members of a commission which would arrange the funeral. The custom in Stalin's Russia was for a "friend" to bury a "friend."

For Khrushchev, this was an important moment, the first time that he had appeared on the national stage closely aligned with Stalin. His appearance meant that whatever the true facts were about Kirov's murder, he must have known them. He must have known which men blamed for the killing were guilty and which were innocent and who had ordered the crime carried out. And twenty-two years later, in his now-famous secret speech denouncing Stalin to the Twentieth Party Congress, Khrushchev would say that when the "mysterious" car accident which killed the witness Borisov occurred, Stalin was already in Stalingrad and that he had already prepared a decree which virtually ordered the execution of anyone charged with anti-Party or anti-State crimes. Of the actual murder, however, Khrushchev spoke vaguely:

It must be asserted that to this day the circumstances surrounding Kirov's murder hide many things which are inexplicable and mysterious and demand a most careful examination. There are reasons for the suspicion that the killer of Kirov, Nikolayev, was assisted by someone from among the people whose duty it was to protect the person of Kirov. A month and a half before the killing, Nikolayev was arrested on the grounds of suspicious behavior, but he was released and not even searched. It is an unusually suspicious circumstance that when the Chekist assigned to protect Kirov was being brought for an interrogation, on December 2, 1934, he was killed in a car "accident" in which no other occupants of the car were harmed. After the murder of Kirov, top functionaries of the Leningrad NKVD were given very light sentences, but in 1937 they were shot. We can assume that they were shot in order to cover the traces of the organizers of Kirov's killing.

In 1956, with Stalin dead, it seemed safe enough to utter such innuendoes and suggestions of guilt. But it was not safe in 1934, and Khrushchev said nothing at the time; he made no objections to the mass arrests or the mass killings.

In fact, the Kirov killing signalled the start of the Great Purge, an orgy of political repression by fear and death. Of the 1,966 delegates to the Congress of Victors, 1,108 were arrested and charged with anti-Party crimes. Of the 139 Members and Candidate Members of the 1934 Central Committee, 98 were executed. The devastations among lesser political functionaries and ordinary citizens were immeasurable; thousands were jailed and thousands more relegated to the bleakness of Sibera. How many were summarily executed will never be known.

With so many lives being snuffed out, numerous opportunities for advancement existed for those who survived. Khrushchev was one of those who benefited. He succeeded Lazar Kaganovich as First Secretary of the Moscow Party and he became a Candidate Member of the Federal Presidium, while holding on to his job as Chief of the Agricultural Political Department. *Pravda* spoke kindly of him in its columns:

N. S. Khrushchev is an outstanding representative of the post-October (Revolution) generation of Party-workers brought up by Stalin.

As his official status was bettered, so were the circumstances of Khrushchev's private life. Several cars were placed at his disposal and special shops supplied items for him and his family that less favored citizens could not buy. He had a larger apartment in Moscow and a dascha—a country home—outside the city. He also had a villa in the Crimea where he could rest from his labors.

Assessing the constantly changing political terrain, Khrushchev realized that those who were able to survive the blood baths would inevitably receive greater authority and rewards. A man of daring and high competence might even attain the ultimate seat of power in the Soviet Union one day. Such visions, however, were never voiced. He was certain that other men entertained the same ideas, men capable of permanently eliminating anyone who appeared to be a competitor for high rank. For the time being, at least, he intended to advance his ambitions cautiously and without attracting attention. A wise man could construct a base of political strength from which to further his cause, make friends and allies in key positions throughout the country and prepare for the struggles that must inevitably come. Khrushchev intended to do exactly that.

Meanwhile, another campaign was under way, a campaign to transform Joseph Stalin into a deity, a god to all the people of the Soviet Union and so to be worshiped and considered a personage who could do no wrong. Khrushchev wasted no time in enlisting in this campaign, thus playing a key role in the "cult of the personality" which he would one day denounce.

Khrushchev searched for opportunities to display his fealty to Stalin and found them. In connection with the trial of Zinoviev and Kamenev, he declaimed with passion:

These men pulled the strings of the bloody plot and aimed a blow at the heart of the Revolution, at thee, our own Stalin, and at thy closest disciples. Damned fascist degenerates. They lifted their hands against the one whose

64

talin (left) and Khrushchev with admirers in 1937.

name millions of toilers speak every day, every hour, with pride and unlimited love . . . Miserable dwarfs. They lifted their hands against the greatest of all men, our friend, our wise leader, Comrade Stalin . . . We promise thee, Comrade Stalin, that the Moscow Bolsheviks—faithful supporters of the Stalinist Central Committee—will sharpen their vigilance still further. They will extirpate what remains of the Trotskyites. They will close ranks . . . around the Stalinist Central Committee and the Great Stalin.

He found other chances to assert his loyalty and orthodoxy. A Bolshevik from Georgia A. S. Yenukidze, holder of several high political posts, made a number of speeches. Studying them, Khrushchev decided that Yenukidze had failed to give enough credit to Stalin for his pre-Revolutionary activities. Khrushchev went onto the attack, and his words were reported in *Pravda:*

The Party showed great trust in Yenukidze, giving him responsible work to do. . . but this did not justify that trust. He betrayed the cause of the revolution. He degenerated politically and morally . . .

Pravda reported that Khrushchev went on to appeal for increased vigilance, for a fight against rotten liberalism and for a greater closing of the ranks of the Moscow Bolsheviks around the Central Committee and the Leader of the Party, Comrade Stalin.

Yenukidze was arrested and shot.

The elimination of such enemies, in accord with Stalin's wishes, barely whetted his appetite. He wanted the Purge carried forward with increased dispatch and efficiency and to this end a telegram was sent to the Politburo:

WE DEEM IT ABSOLUTELY NECESSARY AND URGENT THAT COMRADE YEZHOV BE NOMINATED

TO THE POST OF PEOPLE'S COMMISSAR FOR IN-
TERNAL AFFAIRS. YAGODA HAS DEFINITELY
PROVED HIMSELF TO BE INCAPABLE OF UN-
MASKING THE TROTSKYITE-ZINOVIEVITE BLOC.
THE NKVD IS FOUR YEARS BEHIND IN THIS
MATTER.

Yezhov, Nikolai Ivanovich, was born poor and brought up
hungry. Bitter and resentful, he circulated among Party intellectuals, the writers, the orators, a man unable to speak or write
with force. He was a thin man, frail and small of stature.
Yezhov found much pleasure in this "monster period" of Russia's history, a period that would come to be known as the
Yezhovchina, a time when arrests rose tenfold and thousands of
Russians died, sometimes for little more than leaving their
offices unannounced for a visit to their dentist. Yezhov was the
right man for the job and his terror spread.

Khrushchev could not have been ignorant of Yezhov's activities, nor of anything else that was happening in the Soviet
Union. He moved in a rarefied political atmosphere and made
his contributions to the situation whenever posisble. To him, it
must have seemed necessary, for in the years between 1935 and
1938 seven out of every ten officials at a level of importance
comparable to his were executed. Still others, harried, perse-
cuted and afraid, killed themselves. There were nervous break-
downs and men were tortured in the dismal basement cells of
Lyubyanka prison.

At the start of 1937, thirteen death sentences and a number
of severe prison terms were handed down to members of a
group accused of conspiring against Stalin. In celebration of
the judicial outcome, a meeting was held in Moscow, attended
by two hundred thousand workers. It was Comrade Khrushchev
who delivered the opening speech. He began typically:

Comrade Workers, men and women, engineers, employees, workers of science and art, and all working people of our country! We are gathered here in Red Square to have our proletarian say, to give our full approval of the sentence . . . against the enemies of the people, the traitors of the homeland, the betrayers of the cause of the workers, the spies, the diversionists, the agents of fascism, the villainous, despicable Trotskyites . . .

Here . . . we declare that no matter who attempts to halt our victorious forward sweep toward a Communist society, he will be crushed and destroyed . . .

The betrayers of our homeland . . . who finally faced our proletarian court had for many years struggled against socialism, against the work of Lenin and Stalin. They began with their anti-Leninist "theory" that the building of socialism in one country was impossible, and went on from there to treason against the homeland, to espionage, subversion, terrorism. They became the most despicable lackeys of fascism—that worst enemy of the working class.

. . . The Trotskyite scum dreamed that once again, as before in czarist Russia . . . there would be poverty and hunger for the millions, and riches for a few landowners . . .

Judas Trotsky and his gang wanted to turn over the Ukraine . . . to German and Japanese imperialists, and to transform our flourishing Motherland into a colony of German and Japanese fascism. They wanted to degrade the Russians, Ukrainians, and all other peoples of the U.S.S.R. to the status of a lower race, to be ruled over by the "higher races" of the German and Japanese fascist robbers . . .

The Trotskyites, hoping that the U.S.S.R. would be defeated by the German and Japanese imperialists . . . strove to precipitate . . . war and lay the groundwork for the Soviet defeat. They sabotaged factories with explosions. They killed workers and soldiers. They poisoned children and adults. They derailed trains carrying our fine Red Army soldiers and were paid for this by (foreign) intelligence agents. The Trotskyite murderers thus sold, for money, the blood of the fighters of our valiant army!

There rises from the stench of carrion from the vile, base, Trotskyite degenerates! The verdict against these Trotskyites, these murderers, these agents of fascism, is a warning to all enemies of the people and to all who scheme against our achievements. It is a warning that the working class will, with an iron fist, sweep all enemies of the people off the face of the earth! The foes of mankind, that mad dog, that murderer Trotsky and his lies, are the true agents of the fascists, the incendiaries of a new war.

The language inflamed his listeners and roused fears of hidden and powerful forces at work against them: treachery, subversion and war. To the ordinary people of Russia, for so long victims of selfish and power-hungry masters, this was nothing new. But Comrade Khrushchev was not finished. He had not yet reminded them of where their best interests lay, of their obligations to themselves and to the State. He went on ominously:

These men lifted their villainous hand against Comrade Stalin. By lifting their hand against Comrade Stalin, they lifted it against all of us, against the working class, against the working people. By lifting it against Comrade Stalin, they lifted it against the teachings of Marx, Engels, and Lenin. By lifting their hand against Comrade Stalin, they lifted it against all the best that humanity possesses. For Stalin is hope. He is expectation. He is the beacon that guides all progressive mankind! Stalin is our banner! Stalin is our will! Stalin is our victory!

. . . We must become more vigilant and increase still further our work in all fields of socialist construction, in order to finish off and wipe out all that remains of these vile murderers, fascist agents, Trotskyites, Zinovievites, and their Rightist accomplices.

Twenty years later, Khrushchev would once more turn his attention to the subject of Leon Trotsky, hacked to death in Mexico by one of Stalin's paid assassins, and this time his manner would be tranquil, his words measured, his aims different. This time he said:

> . . . We can speak about the fight against the Trotsky-ites with complete calm. After all, we can name many individuals of great merit who joined the Trotskyites . . . Many of them broke with Trotskyism . . . Was it necessary to annihilate such people? We are deeply convinced that, had Lenin lived, such an extreme method would not have been used against many of them.

His generosity of spirit was two decades too late and hard to accept as genuine despite his final words at the time:

> It is clear that . . . there was no basis for mass terror in the country.

But in 1937 mass terror was the rule of the day, used to destroy all political opposition and to glorify Stalin. Khrushchev knew it, was an integral part of it and intended to profit from it. He soon did.

7

The Purge continued with lengthy public trials that Stalin intended as a continuing indictment of Leon Trotsky. Only those who were willing to "confess" in public were actually put on display; many others had their fates decided before secret tribunals. Forty members of Stalin's personal bodyguard were secretly put on trial. Two were executed; the remainder, imprisoned. The "Man of Steel" enlisted a new bodyguard from his native Georgia.

One trial involved eight top Russian generals who were shot. To help convince the public that they were indeed guilty as charged, their widows were commanded to denounce them as traitors. Those who refused were deported to Siberia.

Though men came and went with startling suddenness in the Soviet Union, Nikita Sergeyevich was unable to advance his private cause. He felt mired down in Moscow, having gone about as far as he could on the local level. Any further advancement would have to be on the national scene. He was already one of the one hundred member Central Committee but the Politburo, the supreme ruling body of the country, had only ten openings and none was vacant. At least not yet.

Appraising the situation with his finely-honed peasant intelligence, Khrushchev concluded that the shortest route to a higher level must inevitably take him away from Moscow, away from the political center of the country but into an arena where he could make a larger, more lasting reputation for himself.

Casting about for a logical place to achieve his purpose, he chose a familiar and potentially rewarding region—the Ukraine. Not only was he acquainted with conditions there, having worked in the area as a young man under Kaganovich, but in the Soviet scheme of things, the Ukraine was a special place. Second largest among Soviet republics, it was economically advanced, the agricultural heart of the nation, and so offered an ambitious Party worker considerable room in which to develop his talents.

There was only one problem; no important jobs were available. But that didn't trouble Khrushchev too much. With the Purge continuing, there was a good chance that that single shortcoming soon would be corrected.

It was. In February, 1937, at a plenary session of the Central Committee, Pavel P. Postyshev, Second Secretary of the Party in the Ukraine, rose to speak. He questioned the need for the Purge, declared his conviction that many of those charged and found guilty were actually innocent and that their confessions were fraudulent.

The members shifted about uneasily. They knew Postyshev to be a man with some popular following, having been instrumental in returning Christmas trees to the children of Russia, after they had been banned for the decade following the Revolution. They knew too that Postyshev, and his colleague and friend Stanislav V. Kossior, First Secretary in the Ukraine, were for increased local independence.

Because of such attitudes, Postyshev had been criticized earlier and relieved of some of his authority. Kossior, because of his friendship with Postyshev, had found himself somewhat discredited.

Now, after questioning the Purge, Postyshev returned to the Ukraine. What he didn't know was that his fate was sealed. A variety of forces were aligned against him, with Khrushchev in the vanguard. Khrushchev told the Fourteenth Ukrainian Party Congress that: "The enemies of the people who sat in the leadership of the Central Committee . . . of the Ukraine . . .

knew very well that the stronger the Party organization, the more dangerous it is to the enemies of the working class and, first of all, to the Polish landlords and the German barons. And there they—the Polish agents . . . did everything in order to weaken the Bolshevik discipline, to corrupt the party organization."

No one could doubt who Khrushchev had in mind. Postyshev and Kossior were the "enemies of the people" and Kossior was of Polish extraction.

It was made clear to Stalin that the Ukraine was in need of fresh leadership, a man, able and dedicated, who would energetically Stalinize the area's forty million people. Soon Postyshev was expelled from the Politburo and subsequently arrested. When he refused to confess to being a traitor, he was shot, and so was Kossior.

Years later Khrushchev would rehabilitate the reputations of both men, saying the charges against them had been contrived, and blaming Stalin for their deaths. But in 1938 Khrushchev offered no objection when he was appointed to fill Postyshev's seat in the Politburo, or no objection when he was made boss of the Ukraine. The Purge had done well by the one-time Donets Basin machinist.

In the maturity of his political life, Khrushchev would try very hard to remove himself from any association with the butchery and political knavery of the Great Purge, claiming ignorance of what had been happening or a minimum of responsibility. The words he spoke in those days, however, indict him. More than passively agreeing with Stalin's cruelty, he actively assisted in spreading the terror and in deifying the "Man of Steel." His speeches reveal his skill as an agitator, words deliberately arranged to arouse his listeners to a frenzy. Aware of what was taking place, he became an integral cog in that lethal machinery and continued to reap rich rewards.

The Ukraine was a large area which shared portions of its

Western frontier with Poland; these have been fought over frequently. Poles, Russians and a Jewish minority composed its population when Khrushchev arrived in Kiev. Most Ukrainians considered Russian rule to be foreign domination, and there was a powerful movement for independence.

Khrushchev was committed to ending all opposition and to advancing a campaign of Russification. In practical terms this meant intensifying the Great Purge against those who opposed Moscow's authority, and those who dared to question the infallibility of Joseph Stalin or the Communist Party.

Khrushchev was especially anxious to eliminate those whom Moscow labelled "bourgeois nationalists"—Ukrainian patriots. Talk of an independent Ukraine was considered more dangerous than ever in light of the rising threat of Nazi Germany in Europe, then creating a powerful war machine under the leadership of Adolf Hitler. But hatred of Russia was so great in the region that many Ukrainians preferred to flee to Germany where they were able to extract promises of freedom for the republic in the near future. All this served to intensify Stalin's desire to subdue the area, and whatever Stalin wanted Khrushchev would do.

Now forty-four years old, Khrushchev had taken a vital step in advancing his career by returning to the Ukraine, though there were those in Moscow who viewed the move as a demotion. Away from the bureaucracy of the Kremlin, he would be able to fully utilize his strengths—his ability as an agitator, for example—and to give full voice to the authority which he knew so well how to use. On his own at last, he would learn how to *govern,* while those he left behind would continue to practice intrigue, dealing only with their own kind. Khrushchev would work with the people, get to understand them and their problems and let them know him. But first he intended to rid the Ukraine of Stalin's enemies.

"Our cause is a holy cause," he announced to the Ukrainian Party Congress. "And he whose hand trembles, who stops half-way, whose knees shake before annihilating ten, a hundred enemies, exposes the Revolution to danger.

"It is necessary to fight the enemies without mercy. Let us erase from the surface of the earth everybody who plans to attack the workers and the peasants. We warn that for every drop of honest workers' blood we will shed a bucketful of the enemy's black blood."

He meant it. He purged and communized, tolerating no opposition as he stepped up a campaign of Russification. Local customs were altered, or eliminated, language was changed and ancient traditions and ceremonies were banned. Any Party member who felt himself to be a nationalist, and acted accordingly, was in danger, and many were killed.

The local chief of the NKVD testified to Khrushchev's ability to suppress all dissident factions. He explained: "I consider myself a pupil of Nikolai Ivanovich Yezhov. Comrade Yezhov teaches us to fight the enemies of the people, to purge our country, our Motherland, of its enemies . . .

"Only after the faithful Stalinist, Nikita Sergeyevich Khrushchev, arrived in the Ukraine did the smashing of the enemies of the people begin in earnest . . ."

In his secret denunciation of Stalin and Stalinism in 1956, Khrushchev would condemn Yezhov's police practices as being degenerate; in 1938 they were precious tools to be utilized by a man advancing himself and faithful to his master.

During all this, Khrushchev managed to further his image as "a man of the people," spending a great deal of his time on industrial and agricultural matters and declaring his concern for the welfare of the ordinary people. He visited collective farms, steel mills, schools, mines and workers' clubs. He talked to students, housewives and peasants. And wherever he went, he preached the virtues of hard work and dedication to Stalin, demanding eternal vigilance against the enemy, those who had "wormed their way into the Party" and aimed at its eventual destruction.

In his new eminence, Khrushchev began to attract attention both wanted and unwanted. Some of it came from Lavrenti Beria, the new chief of the NKVD. A bespectacled man with a professorial appearance, Beria was deeply cruel and blood-thirsty, but more discreet than his predecessors.

In 1939, Beria and Khrushchev clashed for the first time. Five officials of the NKVD in the Ukraine were arrested. All had worked closely with Khrushchev and now confessions were forced from them incriminating their superiors, namely Nikita Sergeyevich Khrushchev.

Such testimony was placed in so-called "black files," for use when and if the official implicated should incur the anger of Joseph Stalin. The files contained reports of Khrushchev's "excesses" since coming to the Ukraine.

Another man might have panicked, admitted his failings and begged forgiveness. Not Khrushchev. He viewed the situation coolly and decided that there was no immediate threat. No matter what Beria did or said, Stalin was satisfied with Khru-shchev and his work and knew that his loyalty was deep and steady. How right he was became clear to everyone that same year when he was made a full member of the Politburo, one of the eight rulers of the Party, and the country—under Stalin.

As dictator in the Ukraine, Khrushchev was feared and hated. He was riding in a railroad car with two of his subordinates, later in the year, when his lofty place in the Communist order was dramatically noted by Ukrainian nationalists. A bomb was heaved through a window. Khrushchev escaped with minor injuries, but his two colleagues were killed.

Elsewhere, events were happening that would affect nations and people everywhere in the world. In the summer of 1939, Maxim Litvinov, Commissar for Foreign Affairs since 1930, was removed from office by Stalin who judged Litvinov's policy of collective security a failure. He was replaced by Vyacheslav Molotov, an old friend of the dictator's. Then, on August 25, the people of the world were shocked to learn that Communist

Khrushchev talks to the people of Kiev shortly after its liberation from the Nazis.

Russia, archenemy of Fascism, had concluded a non-aggression pact with Nazi Germany.

The treaty was made with the approval of the Politburo, and its members were told that a secret clause provided Russia with a free hand to do as she wished in Finland, the Baltic States and Eastern Poland. This pact allowed Hitler to concentrate his aggressive moves against the nations of Western Europe, confident that the USSR would not come to their defense.

To Nikita Khrushchev this meant his responsibility was to absorb sections of Eastern Poland into the Ukraine, to pacify them and to Russify them.

He went right to work, creating a Ukrainian military command under Semyon Timoshenko. Khrushchev also was supported by the young and very able Ivan Alexandrovich Serov, leader of the Ukrainian NKVD, beginning a long and mutually profitable relationship. Serov was a happy man, without too much ambition, content to inflict the mass terror and cruelty that fell to a man in his job.

On September 1, 1939, his rear now secure from Russian attack, Hitler turned his booted legions loose on Poland. The Poles fought back.

In the Ukraine, preparations were accelerated to occupy the eastern portion of its beleaguered neighbor. On September 17, the Red Army marched. More accurately, it flew and it floated. Thousands of parachutists were dropped into the desired territory, and, in only three days, the occupation was completed. A propaganda leaflet distributed among the Poles and signed by Khrushchev and Timoshenko, claimed that the Red Army had marched into what it termed the "Western Ukraine" in order to liberate the people ". . . from the landowners and generals, from the enemy that wants to destroy you, while we stretch out our hand to the Western Ukrainian brothers . . . The Red Army will wipe off the face of the earth anyone who stands in the way of the gigantic historic deed of liberating our brothers."

Thanks to Comrade Khrushchev's efficient planning, the occupation went smoothly. He had overlooked nothing, organized everything and everyone, including a Political Division created to Russify the new lands.

Within the first month, all hostile elements in Eastern Poland were destroyed. Under orders from Khrushchev, Serov commenced the deportation of "enemies of the people," those who were bourgeois nationalists: shopkeepers, priests, socialists and businessmen. The Polish Communist Party, too independent for the requirements of the Kremlin, was swiftly decimated. Truck convoys and freight trains were packed with these unfortunate people who were transported to prisons and to newly built concentration camps. About a million and a half Poles were sent to labor camps in Siberia. The officer corps of the Polish Army and many intellectuals were arrested as attempts were made to "disinfect" the area from the taint of capitalism. Six hundred thousand Jews were also deported.

Meanwhile, thousands of Polish soldiers were in flight from Hitler's Panzer Divisions, picking their way eastward in hope of finding safety. They discovered none. Communist doctrine made no provision for their survival, and many of them died of illness or starvation. Ten thousand Polish officers were eventually shot by the NKVD, most of them in the Katyn forest which was under Khrushchev's jurisdiction, though he had no direct connection with this massacre.

On June 28, 1940, the Red Army invaded the disputed regions of Bukovina and Bessarabia in Rumania, making them part of the Ukraine ". . . by virtue of history, language and national composition . . ."

Once again Khrushchev worked hard to absorb the new lands and new people into his domain. He agitated for socialization of industry and commerce and for collective farming. At the same time, he instituted security measures to protect the growing Ukraine Republic from subversive elements and foreign spies. Thus he gained experience in ruling a large country, dealing with all aspects of its economy and social structure, its institutions and its people; experience that would prove invaluable in future years.

Operation Barbarossa was its code name, the Nazi invasion of Russia. British Intelligence discovered the plan, and Prime Minister Winston Churchill sent a warning to Joseph Stalin. The Soviet dictator refused to believe it. Here, he and other leading Communists were certain, was another trick to embroil Russia in a bloody war with Germany to the profit of the imperialists. He anticipated that England, then fighting Germany, would soon conclude a peace pact with Hitler, and so the warning was ignored.

Other warnings fell on equally deaf ears. Information came from Russian Army commanders, from deserters from the German army and from diplomats. General Korponos, Chief of the Kiev Special Military District, wrote directly to Stalin saying that the Germans were massing at the Nazi-Russian frontier in Poland, and suggesting that defensive measures be instituted. Stalin's reply was that nothing was to be done lest Germany be provoked.

On June 22, 1941, Germany attacked Russia. On that same day, Khrushchev was in Moscow. He hurried back to Kiev to oversee the defenses there.

Russia was in desperate trouble. The Nazi war machine sliced across a seven hundred mile front as if unopposed, penetrating deep into the country, seemingly unstoppable. And at the eastern edge of the Soviet Union, the Japanese, Germany's allies, were poised, ready to pounce at the strategic moment.

Stalin was shaken by this unexpected turn of events. He refused to accept the evidence of his senses and wouldn't believe that war had begun. Orders were issued that German gunfire was *not* to be returned for fear it would provoke and anger the Nazis. Stalin insisted that the outbreaks were local, the efforts of a few dissident units. As a result, a large portion of

Soviet military strength was destroyed along the borders, and many officers and men died unnecessarily.

Khrushchev, too, was stunned. Everything he had worked for and accomplished was on the verge of disaster. The nation seemed without defenses, destined to be looted and raped, laid to waste, conquered. But unlike Stalin, Khrushchev was not immobilized. It was not his nature to accept defeat passively.

Back in the Ukraine, he went to work with all the energy stored in his muscular frame. He became deeply involved in all operations, political, economic and military. He put phone calls through to the Kremlin, to the new Foreign Minister and to Malenkov.

"People have volunteered for the new army and demand arms," he said. "You must send us arms."

"We cannot," Malenkov replied coldly. "We are sending all our rifles to Leningrad and you have to arm yourselves."

In his 1956 denunciation of Stalin, Khrushchev referred to this time, saying: "Had our industry been mobilized properly and in time to supply the army with the necessary material, our wartime losses would have been decidedly smaller. Such mobilization had not been, however, started in time. And already in the first days of the war it became evident that our army was badly armed, that we did not have enough artillery, tanks, and planes to throw the enemy back . . ."

Khrushchev labored long hours, completely involved in the fight. Under attack, the Soviet Union gathered all its resources to repel the invaders. Factories, businesses, supplies, livestock and heavy equipment—all were evacuated to safe areas in order to deny them to the advancing Germans. As the Nazis occupied whole sections of the Ukraine, Khrushchev moved to thwart them, establishing a partisan army to fight behind the lines. This was organized along Communist Party lines with direct communications open to Khrushchev so he could maintain effective control.

Holding the rank of lieutenant general, and considered an

expert on evacuation, Khrushchev was placed in charge of the evacuation of Stalingrad. He shipped entire factories, entire civilian populations, all farm animals and equipment further east. And, during the winter of 1942-43, he was in charge of partisan activities in that area.

Living close to the fighting, experiencing the cruelty of war and those special horrors which the Germans reserved for the Russians, Khrushchev viewed Nazi barbarism first-hand. He saw cities and villages destroyed, the ravaged landscape, the millions of men, women and children who were beaten, burned, tortured and shot; twenty million dead in all. His eldest son, Leonid, was killed during the defense of Stalingrad.

With the help of American arms and equipment, Russia fought back. By the close of 1943, the Ukraine had been cleared of Germans, and Khrushchev was again in charge of that republic.

With the war still being fought—Soviet armies were pushing the Germans back, as were the soldiers of the United States and England in the West—and patriotism still firing most Russians, Khrushchev was able to return to his primary tasks: organizing a country of forty million people and rebuilding the political, economic and cultural life of the Ukraine. In addition to being First Secretary, he had been appointed by Stalin to be Chairman of the Ukrainian Council of Commissars. At once he held an unprecedented mass of personal power with absolute authority over the richest province in the Soviet Union—under Stalin, of course.

8

At last the war was over; the horror of Nazi conquest and occupation, repelled. But much of the Soviet Union had been devastated and there was much to be repaired, replaced and reclaimed. The mines had to be pumped dry; the factories rebuilt; workers gathered and trained. The ruined land had once again to be made fertile. There was a need for everything—tools, farming equipment, industrial machinery, transportation of every kind, grain, fertilizer, seed, lumber, cement. Everything.

Much of this was available in the world outside of Russia's borders, particularly in the United States which had been physically untouched by the war and was thriving. The Soviet Union had only to ask for what she needed and her ally probably would have supplied it. Stalin decided not to ask.

A great scheme had come to his mind, a scheme that would permit him to annex a considerable portion of Eastern and Central Europe. Stalin understood that the West viewed Soviet military power with a certain amount of awe, and had been deeply impressed by the spirited defense of Russia. He planned to exploit this reaction.

Bluster, bluff and blackmail were the weapons the "Man of Steel" intended to wield against his former allies, weapons paid for by the Russian people. Weary and wounded by the terrible war—ten million young Russian soldiers and another ten million civilians had died in the fighting—cities levelled and farms ravaged, the people, for the first time in their history, stood firmly in support of the government, and Stalin intended to profit from that singular condition.

He accurately assessed the temper of his people and that of the West. His former allies, tired of war and armies, quickly disbanded their huge fighting forces and directed their energies to peaceful endeavors. Here was Stalin's chance to spread the rule of Hammer and Sickle and he did so, sacrificing goods and services for his people in order to maintain and strengthen his military establishment.

Concerned by Russian aggressiveness, demands and threats, the Western nations began to reestablish their armories, including the development of nuclear weapons. Stalin reacted typically, and once again Russians lacked enough food so that the Red Army could arm itself with nuclear bombs and rockets. Ten long years after the end of World War II, Russia was unable to produce shoes enough for all its people—but the Soviets were the first to put a man in space.

All the shortages and difficulties of life in post-war Russia existed in the Ukraine, with some added local flourishes. There were, Nikita Sergeyevich Khrushchev discovered soon after his return, roving bands of Ukrainian rebels who resisted Russian occupation, striking against the authorities, killing and looting. They had to be put down, and Khrushchev turned that assignment over to Beria's NKVD and units of the Red Army, which took several years to complete the job.

That he was forced to work against continuing violence troubled Khrushchev, making his task that much more difficult. Such complications forced him to intensify his efforts as he labored to reestablish the Ukraine as a prosperous and peaceful region, and once again to assert his authority there.

He was deeply committed to welding the province closer to Moscow and to its Russification. Part of the process was to purge all undesirable elements. There was one other task he gave himself which was the most dangerous of all—the personal glorification of Nikita Khrushchev. Here was a project that demanded the most delicate touch, for he remembered vividly that his predecessors, Postyshev and Kossior, had been tumbled from power, in part, because of precisely that kind of activity.

But Khrushchev, always the cunning, pragmatic man was ideally equipped to deal with the realities of Soviet politics. Launching his campaign of self-promotion, he was careful never to intrude on Joseph Stalin's preeminence in all things. Posters appeared in towns and villages everywhere in the Ukraine bearing Khrushchev's likeness; there were paintings and even sculptures, but always Stalin's image was alongside. Khrushchev realized that, in this way, he accomplished two things: he catered to the bloated ego of the man in the Kremlin and, in the minds of the people, he was becoming solidly associated with the premier figure in the country.

Khrushchev had been moving in this direction for some time. As early as 1944, he had arranged for a collective of thirteen well-known Ukrainian writers to compose a poem titled, "To the Great Stalin from the Ukrainian People." A lengthy work, it bore the signed endorsement of 9,316,973 people. The first stanza read:

> Today and forever, oh, Stalin be praised
> For the light that the plants and the fields
>   do emit!
> Thou art the heart of the people, the truth and
>   the faith!
> We're thankful to Thee for the sun Thou hast lit!

Whether on order or by choice, the poets were careful not to omit Khrushchev from this paean of glory:

> Kiev is free, will remain so for ages,
> Our land, our Mother, salutes it with cheer,

85

Khrushchev and Vatutin, brave and courageous,
Lead forward the armies who fight without fear.

We're united and solid, and no one will dare,
To touch our young land which is clean as
    first love,
As fresh and as young with his silver-gray hair,
Is Stalin's companion, Nikita Khrushchev.

Nor was that the end of it. Five years afterwards, a volume published in Kiev, included these verses:

We are the great foundation
That is the summit's base,
On the ancient Kiev elevation
I see Khrushchev's fine face.

And if my eyes look higher,
I see our Lenin, the foreseer,
The truth and power that inspire,
And Stalin's glorious name I hear.

When he subsequently denounced the cult of Stalinism and the deification of the "Man of Steel," Khrushchev would conveniently forget these as well as other fawning efforts on his part.

None of this was lost to other ambitious men in the apparatus, some of whom recognized Khrushchev as an emerging rival who would eventually have to be defeated in the struggle for power. Much of that intramural squabbling was inspired by Stalin himself, his aim being to maintain uncertainty among his followers, to create unrest and force them to look only to him for strength and rewards. Frequently, he arranged matters so that certain officials discovered other men intruding on their authority and there often were clashes between them.

A Ukrainian farm being harvested by a troika or three-horse team.

Such was the case when Georgi Malenkov, who was only a candidate for membership in the Politburo, was made Chairman of the Governmental Committee on the Restoration of the Economy in Liberated Areas. That imposing title meant that he had authority over Khrushchev in the Ukraine. Since Nikita Sergeyevich had been a member of the Politburo since 1938, he grew resentful.

There were other men rising in the hierarchy, who were a challenge to Khrushchev simply by their existence. One was Andrei Zhdanov who came out of the war as a colonel general and chief of the Leningrad Party. He was influential in Stalin's secretariat. There was Bulganin, a member of the key State Defense Committee and Deputy Commissar of Defense. There was Beria, now a Deputy Prime Minister, who had a shrewdly placed personal following. He was in charge of nuclear development. There were Kaganovich, Molotov, Mikoyan, Voroshilov and others, a company of tough, shrewd political infighters. Rivalries developed and competitors sometimes joined forces for mutual gain, anxious to defeat a common enemy. Malenkov, Zhdanov and Beria were among those who formed such a coalition designed to halt Khrushchev's steady rise before he became too powerful.

Another complication for Khrushchev was that Andrei A. Andreyev was chief of all agricultural policy in the Soviet Union. This allowed him to pry into the Ukraine where agriculture was considered the republic's strongpoint.

Khrushchev had dedicated himself more to improving farming than to anything else, yet ironically it was in this area that he proved most vulnerable to criticism. Not even his boundless energy could prevent a drought in 1946 that brought about a bad harvest. As a result, grain quotas went unfulfilled, and the shortage was felt throughout the land.

Andreyev saw this as his big chance and struck the first blow against Khrushchev early in 1947. He issued a detailed report on Soviet farming to the Central Committee in which he criticized local chieftains for not meeting production standards and pointed to the Ukraine as a prime offender for ". . . serious lagging behind in the production of spring wheat."

Andreyev insisted that it was "intolerable that such a valuable food crop as spring wheat had been neglected year after year in the collective and state farms of the Ukrainian S.S.R., while the fertile black-earth soils were sown with less valuable crops, especially barley." He was also unhappy about the drop in production and delivery of tobacco, sugar beets and other crops.

These were serious charges and, for the most part, unanswerable. Khrushchev was forced to accept them in silence and to await the official wrath. When it came, it was more severe than he had expected. First, he was deposed as chief of the Ukrainian Party. That job was done by his old patron, Lazar Kaganovich, a detail Khrushchev would not forget.

Stunned and angry, he attempted to fight back in the way he knew best, to place the blame elsewhere. "How did it happen?" he asked. "How could it have happened that the sowing of spring wheat was neglected year after year?" To him the answer was obvious: ". . . because this important crop was underestimated. The fault lies primarily with the Ministry of Agriculture." The tactic failed this time, because it was effective only when used in a position of strength. At age fifty-two, after a career that had moved steadily upwards for twenty-five years, Khrushchev seemed to be slipping.

Matters got worse. He was removed from his job in the Kiev Provincial Party Committee, supposedly at his own request. Two days later, he lost his position in the Kiev City Party Committee. Khrushchev did not quite become one of the "unpersons," written out of existence in Soviet histories and encyclopedias for crimes or errors; however from May to September, 1947, his name was never mentioned in a Ukrainian newspaper. He did not attend the session of the Supreme Soviet nor the plenary session of the Ukrainian Central Committee.

There was open speculation about his ability to cling to his seat in the Politburo.

But keep it he did, and more. Owning tremendous political resilience, he did not remain down for very long. In the fall of the year, he resumed his job as First Secretary in the Ukraine, thus becoming a power in the republic again. That his enemies had been unable to finish him off may be explained by recalling the excellent relationship he had built with Joseph Stalin. Had the dictator wanted him removed permanently, it would have been done. Kaganovich, too, must have played an important role in this; he had always been impressed with Khrushchev's organizational ability and viewed him as a victim of circumstance, rather than inefficient, or something worse.

Back in power, Khrushchev launched himself energetically to the task of recollectivizing those collectives which had been dissolved during the German occupation. He was successful, and soon impressive amounts of grain were coming out of the Ukraine.

Armed now with new prestige, he began to reward those followers who had remained loyal to him during his period of disfavor. He promoted many of them and provided other rewards, thus creating an extended power base from which to operate when the right time came.

Aware that he had achieved the maximum advantage from his rule in the Ukraine, and that the fountainhead of power was still Moscow, Khrushchev decided that the time had come to return. He owned a degree of experience few of his rivals could match and was equipped to deal with the questions all rulers must eventually be confronted with and answer. He knew how to deal with people, their needs and their idiosyncrasies; he knew how to wield power. Moreover, if he were ever going to reach the pinnacle, it would have to be soon; at fifty-five he was fifteen years Stalin's junior. The time to make his move had come.

Inevitably it was his agricultural experience that brought him back to Moscow where he was made First Party Secretary, one of five secretaries of the All-Union Central Committee.

Khrushchev returned to find Malenkov an important man in the capital city, with Lavrenti Beria only a step or two behind. Molotov continued to play a key role in political matters and, important also were Kaganovich, Kliment Voroshilov and Andreyev, still a strong man, scheming and distrustful. Others, too, were coming up but had yet to reach a threatening level.

Andreyev, however, posed immediate difficulties. As head of all Soviet farm production, Andreyev worked for a policy of decentralization, with each collective running its own affairs. Khrushchev deliberately came out with an opposing idea, suggesting that collective farmers be resettled in agricultural cities where their labor could be more effectively utilized.

When *Pravda* published an article attacking Andreyev for his position, it repudiated a position the Party had endorsed as far back as 1939. Khrushchev came out in praise of the article and heightened his attacks with a great deal of success. Soon the rapid merger of many small collective farms was completed. Khrushchev declared that ". . . in many collective farms the collective farmers express the desire to unite and create economically powerful collective farms." He claimed that the Party had the responsibility to ". . . assist the collective farmers in carrying out this measure."

By mid-1950, the number of collective farms in the Moscow area had shrunk from 6,069 to 1,668, strong evidence that farmers had little desire to collectivize further. But they were given little choice.

Khrushchev continued to strive for the agricultural city plan with indifferent success. Eventually it was put aside, a defeat that drew criticism from Malenkov before a Party Congress.

"It should be noted," he said acidly, "that certain of our leading officials have indulged in a wrong approach, a consumer's approach, to problems of collective farm development, particularly in connection with carrying out the amalgamation of small collective farms . . . these comrades overlooked . . . the major tasks—the tasks of production."

It would take more than such mild criticism to slow Khrushchev now. He battled and schemed to maintain his place close to Stalin, being careful not to be pushed into a political corner and trapped, picking his way carefully along the dangerous path he had chosen to travel.

At fifty-six, Khrushchev had been transformed into the personality the entire world would eventually come to know. Almost totally bald, he was aggressive, inordinately sure of himself, sometimes drunk—sometimes sober, laughing exuberantly or savagely angry. He could be an overpowering bully, scornful of anyone who displeased him and boastful of his own abilities and accomplishments, yet fully capable of enacting the role of a helpless pleader for causes in which he believed. He was a compulsive talker, a compulsive worker, a plotter of limitless skills, who viewed the world through tiny eyes that squinted as if he were trying to see beyond his limitations. He was a man who knew what he wanted and intended to get it.

At seventy, Joseph Stalin was considered by many of his close associates to be on the edge of senility, his once sharp brain dull and unreliable. He was a man suffering from paranoia. If Khrushchev agreed with this diagnosis, he gave no sign. Instead, to celebrate Stalin's birthday, he authored a pamphlet titled: "Stalin-Friendship Among the Peoples Makes Our Motherland Invincible." In it he characterized the dictator as ". . . the wise father of peoples," decorating this accolade with a string of laudatory comments. Stalin, he wrote, had won "freedom and independence for Hungary, Czechoslovakia, Poland, Rumania, Bulgaria, and Albania" and ". . . millions of people turn with the deepest love and devotion toward Stalin . . . Glory to our dear father, wise teacher, genius, and leader . . . Comrade Stalin."

Only six years later, Khrushchev would issue a strong condemnation of the ". . . most dissolute flattery . . ." that certain persons had heaped upon the "Man of Steel."

Khrushchev had learned to accept the inevitable when it occurred and so, with the defeat of his agricultural cities plan, he looked elsewhere to further his ambitions. No place offered more promise of high reward than the Communist Party itself, repository of all power in the Soviet Union, next to Stalin himself. This, then, was to be his next field of operations, his avenue to greater success.

As if anticipating this, and always anxious to solidify his own authority, Stalin imposed his will on the Party. He renamed the Politburo, calling it the Party Presidium, and it was expanded from ten to twenty-five members. This diluted the power of each member, including Khrushchev, as the Party itself was downgraded and Stalin's hold on it strengthened.

9

In January, 1953, an official communiqué was tucked inconspicuously in the last column of *Pravda's* last page. It read:

Soviet security organs uncovered some time ago a terrorist group of physicians, who, by prescribing harmful treatment, sought to cut short the lives of the Soviet leaders.

Nine doctors were named, all of whom were attached to the Kremlin, and they were accused of having poisoned several prominent persons whom they had treated, among them Andrei Zhdanov, who had died five years earlier. The doctors were accused, too, of making false diagnoses and so injuring the well-being of Soviet leaders. Added to this, was the charge of practicing faulty treatment.

Seven of the nine doctors were Jews and they were specifically accused of being involved with ". . . a Zionist espionage organization working for the American secret service." The Jewish Professors of Medicine, it was claimed, poisoned Zhdanov, and others, and were planning to poison a number of Red Army leaders including Marshals Govorov, Koniev and Vassilevsky.

Only a year before, Professor Vinogradov, one of the Jewish doctors accused, had been honored with the Order of Lenin. Now he was put to endless questioning and torture; two of his colleagues died during the process.

This "plot" erupted upon the Soviet scene with stunning impact. Russians had long been accustomed to plots and counterplots, intrigue and murder. The Czars had used such techniques to maintain their power and there had been little change since the Bolsheviks had come to power; people recalled that Trotsky had actually accused Stalin of doing away with Lenin.

Soon after the revelation of the doctors' plot, the security apparatus, under S. D. Ignatiev, who was ultimately responsible to Lavrenti Beria, was criticized for tardiness in uncovering the scheme. Here was a message that all high officials in the USSR understood without difficulty—a new purge was in the making, directed against Beria's security organization, as well as all others whom Stalin distrusted.

Anyone might now fall victim to the dictator's suspicions, for these days he perceived enemies everywhere and viewed the slightest deviation from his personal whim as a threat. Three years later, in his secret speech, Khrushchev would refer pointedly to these uncertain days:

Let us also recall the "affair of the doctor-plotters." Actually there was no "affair" outside the declaration of the woman doctor Timashuk, who was probably influenced or ordered by someone (after all, she was an official collaborator of the organs of State Security) to write Stalin a letter in which she declared that doctors were applying supposedly improper methods of medical treatment.

Such a letter was sufficient for Stalin to reach an immediate conclusion that there are doctor-plotters in the Soviet Union . . .

He said that Academician Vinogradov should be put in chains, that another one should be beaten. Present at this Congress as a delegate is the former Minister of State Security, Comrade Ignatiev. Stalin told him curtly: "If you do not obtain confessions from the doctors we will shorten you by a head.

Stalin personally called the investigative judge, gave him instructions . . .

. . . Stalin told us: "You are blind like young kittens;

what will happen without me? The country will perish because you do not know how to recognize enemies . . ."

When we examined this "case" . . . , we found it to be fabricated from beginning to end.

An atmosphere of personal and national concern was created by all this among the Party and Government hierarchy. Obviously, Stalin might strike out in any direction at any time, name any man as an enemy of the people, that vague but damning phrase against which there was no defense. Some Soviet leaders began to think—but never to utter those thoughts—that Stalin had gone mad, had lost all touch with reality and was insanely determined to pull the entire governmental structure down around him. Of this, Khrushchev said in 1956:

> Because of his extreme suspicion, Stalin toyed also with the absurd and ridiculous suspicion that Voroshilov was an English agent. It's true—an English agent! A special tapping device was installed in his home to listen to what was said there.
>
> By unilateral decision Stalin also separated one other man from the work of the Political Bureau, Andreyevich Andreyev . . . one of the most unbridled acts of willfulness.
>
> . . . It is not excluded that had Stalin remained at the helm for another several months Comrades Molotov and Mikoyan would probably have not delivered any speeches at this Congress.
>
> Stalin evidently had plans to finish off the old members of the Political Bureau.

Khrushchev was convinced that had the situation been continued, Kaganovich would have been driven out of the apparatus along with Beria. Malenkov, also, would have been removed since he functioned closely with Beria. How far might such a purge have gone if men of such eminence were suspected and in danger? At that time, the newspapers were studded with scare stories, and the radio shrilled out its warnings—"Vigilance! Beware of Spies!"

That the purge did not get out of hand and spread more widely, Khrushchev attributed to *his* opposition, and that of other top leaders who stood against Stalin in this matter. He said that there would have been many more victims ". . . if everyone who worked beside Stalin at that time had agreed with him in everything." Stalin intended to create ". . . the so-called case of the Moscow counter-revolutionary centre. But as is known, he found no yes-men . . ."

Perhaps. But Stalin did not have to concern himself with open opposition from any of his colleagues, though they may not have provided the total cooperation he desired.

As 1953 moved into February, confidence in Stalin was waning. Khrushchev, no longer the unsophisticated peasant of his youth, his intelligence sharpened by years of experience in war and in peace, was able to understand what was happening around him. He was equipped to decide what had to be done for the good of his country, and for his own good. But fate eliminated any need for action.

Eight years earlier, returning to Russia from his meeting in Teheran with Winston Churchill and President Roosevelt, Stalin had suffered a slight stroke. Now, on March 2, 1953, the "Man of Steel" was again afflicted.

The news shocked Khrushchev. On the previous Saturday, he had visited Stalin's dacha, with other Soviet leaders, where he had enjoyed a fine dinner and a pleasant evening. Stalin had been in good spirits, full of energy and life. On Sunday, Khrushchev did not receive the usual phone call from the dictator. That was odd, but not worrisome. Then on Monday, Stalin failed to show up at his office in the Kremlin, and that evening his personal bodyguard called to announce that the "Man of Steel" was ill.

Khrushchev sped out to the dacha, as did Beria, Malenkov,

Bulganin and others. They found Stalin unconscious, partially paralyzed by a blood clot, and attended by a team of physicians. Khrushchev later reported that after three days Stalin ". . . came out of his coma and we went into his room. A nurse was feeding him with a spoon. He shook us by the hand and tried to joke with us, smiling feebly and waving his good arm to a picture over his bed of a baby lamb being fed with a spoon by a little girl. Now, he indicated by gestures, he was just as helpless as a baby lamb."

On March 4, a medical bulletin alerted the world to the gravity of the situation. Stalin's suffering in those last days was intense, and the doctors applied leeches and gave him injections in an effort to make it easier for him. But his breathing grew more labored and the pain increased. At ten minutes before ten o'clock on the evening of March 5, Stalin died.

"I wept," Khrushchev said. "After all, we were his pupils and owed him everything. Like Peter the Great, Stalin fought barbarism with barbarism, but he was a great man."

A communiqué was issued:

The heart of Lenin's comrade-in-arms and the inspired continuer of Lenin's cause, the wise teacher and the leader of the Party and the people has stopped beating. . . . Our task is to guard . . . the steel-like and monolithic unity of the Party as the apple of our eye . . . to educate all Communists and toiling people in high political vigilance, irreconcilability and firmness in the struggle against inner and outer foes . . . the most important task of the Party and the government is to ensure . . . the greatest unity of leadership and the prevention of any kind of disorder and panic.

Panic and disorder. These were what the hierarchy feared so much. They warned the people not to panic when they themselves were so close to it. Having dispensed terror and death for

Khrushchev is second from the left in the honor guard at Stalin's bier.

so long, having lived with Stalin's cruel rule, and abetting it, they quaked at what might happen now. How would the citizens of the Soviet Union, the Red Army, the satellite countries, and the capitalist world react? There was danger everywhere. The Cold War was then at its peak and none of them could say with certainty that it might not break out into a shooting war with nuclear weapons being used. And there was always the possibility of a popular revolt.

In the streets of Moscow, people wept at the announcement of Stalin's death. Were they tears of joy or of anguish? No one knew for sure.

One thing was certain; the new Soviet leadership intended to take no chances. The people in the capital city discovered that the streets were sealed off by tanks and armored cars, and Beria's troopers were everywhere, armed and ready. The commander of the city's military district as well as the commandants of the Moscow City garrison and the Kremlin guards were arrested. Nothing was overlooked in the desire of the hierarchy to protect themselves, to prevent any moves against them.

Still gripped by uncertainty and distrust, the leaders collected behind the crenelated Kremlin walls to arrange the future of the nation and themselves.

It was a stimulating and exciting time for Khrushchev. The shrewd peasant intelligence was alert, perceptive, anxious to miss nothing. The tiny eyes darted here and there, seeking evidence of this one's attitude, that one's aspirations and remembering weaknesses noted earlier.

He recognized at once that fear was the dominating emotion of the day, and that much of it was directed toward him. His colleagues had long ago recognized his strength and drive, his ability to get things done and to move close to the people, qualities most of them lacked.

Khrushchev understood fear and its uses; he also understood the importance of reassuring the others that he presented no threat to any of them; at least, not yet. Collective leadership was what was needed and he said so, speaking in favor of whatever government might be formed. He aimed to convince the others that he had no intention of trying to step into Stalin's shoes, of making himself a dictator. Nikita Sergeyevich, his words made clear, was a threat to no one, a man in the rear ranks, a man to be trusted.

Helping project this image was the fact that he had never achieved the *public* stature of a Malenkov, a Beria, a Molotov. He was a man in the shadows, relatively unknown outside the Kremlin, even to the great mass of Russians.

Adding to his advantage was the view of his peers that, as a man who got things done, he was willing to work tirelessly under the leadership of someone else. True, he had vied with others for advancement and for favor from Stalin, but so had they all. And Khrushchev had always subordinated his own thoughts to those of the man at the top. They were certain he would continue to do so.

What they couldn't know was that at last, at age fifty-nine, Khrushchev was ready to become his own man, to step into the bright glare of political sunshine and to make his move toward total power. To do this he intended to utilize both his friends and his enemies.

Less than one hour after the announcement of Stalin's death, a special committee to make the funeral arrangements was named. Nikita Sergeyevich was appointed its chairman. Perhaps those who chose him for the honor forgot that nineteen years earlier Joseph Stalin had organized the funeral of his predecessor, Lenin.

This done, Stalin's heirs turned to the important business of establishing a succession of rule to suit themselves. Among men who considered themselves equals, this meant terminating much of the former suspicious dealing and plotting.

First, five members of the Secretariat were summarily fired.

101

Next, the Presidium, which Stalin had enlarged in order to weaken its authority, was reduced to fourteen members. Government ministries were cut from fifty-two to twenty-five.

Malenkov was named Premier and chief of the Party, with Molotov, Beria, Kaganovich and Bulganin acting as First Deputy Prime Ministers. To please the Red Army, Marshal Grigori Zhukov was reclaimed from the obscurity to which Stalin had condemned him and made Deputy Minister of Defense. The new Secretariat was composed of Malenkov, Khrushchev, Suslov, Pospelov, Shatalin and Ignatiev, the same man criticized by Stalin for failing to uncover the doctors' plot sooner. Two of Stalin's favorites, Alexei Kosygin and Leonid Brezhnev (at this writing Premier and President respectively of the USSR), were excluded by Malenkov.

All was not yet settled. On the day after Stalin's funeral, Malenkov began to slip from his position of power. The press paid less attention to him and quoted him less frequently. Three days later it became apparent to those who could read the signs that he no longer controlled the Party. Collective leadership was a popular idea and the phrase was heard again and again. The Central Committee and the Presidium were emphasized and it was clear that Comrade Malenkov was not running the country. All this pleased Khrushchev as he worked behind the scenes to win friends and allies for his personal cause.

Khrushchev, as Second Secretary, directed the Central Committee, the only one of the five secretaries who was also a member of the Presidium. He was careful to retain the friendship of the others and all of them were allied against Beria. None of them could forget how promptly his police and soldiers moved into Moscow on the night of Stalin's death. His raw ambition for power troubled them, and they feared what could happen if he were to take Stalin's place.

The jockeying for advantage continued, and mistakes were inevitably made, but not by Nikita Khrushchev. Since no one suspected he yearned for the premier's job, no alliances were made against him and he was able to operate unhindered. Moving cautiously, he drew no unwanted attention, never pushed too hard. Instead he spoke and acted only in the name of the Party, the Central Committee, the "Leninist Collective Leadership." He played it safe, and smart.

Khrushchev had achieved a unique status—he held dual positions in the Party, something of which no other leader could boast. He was a member of the Presidium, the policy-making body, and one of five in the Secretariat, the Party's executive arm. Most important, under his leadership, the Party co-existed with the Government and in this way he had managed to quietly neutralize Malenkov's authority. Pleased with the way things were going, Khrushchev was able now to take time to assess the political situation, to note who stood between him and complete power—Molotov, Bulganin, Beria and his old patron, Lazar Kaganovich. All of them, Khrushchev decided privately, would have to go.

An inevitable outgrowth of collective leadership was a slackening of official controls, an increasing freedom for the people. Writers, poets and other intellectuals, long suppressed in Russia, began to speak out on political matters, daring to voice positions not officially approved. No one criticized Stalin, of course, but he was ignored for the most part, relegated to the back benches of history.

For Khrushchev, this was a good time and he worked feverishly to place his supporters, many of them Ukrainians, in key positions throughout the country, thereby establishing a personal apparatus. He worked carefully and skillfully avoided creating friction or arousing fears.

As part of this new freedom, a widespread amnesty was announced in March under which certain categories of convicts and concentration camp inmates were to be released. These included mothers of children under the age of ten, pregnant women, children under eighteen, old people and those whose sentences were for fewer than five years. Others had their sentences halved. Excluded were those in jail for counter-revolutionary activities or for embezzling large amounts of money.

The amnesty shocked the people of Russia. Here was official recognition that pregnant women, mothers and children had been locked away in concentration camps and in prisons. The amnesty was a thinly veiled attack on Beria and his secret police.

As if to protect himself by establishing his own liberal stance, Beria publicly exposed the doctors' plot as a fraud with the result that the physicians involved were declared innocent and freed. Only then was it learned that not nine but fifteen doctors had been imprisoned. Beria had to blame someone for what had happened and he named the former Minister of State Security Ignatiev, and his deputy, Ryumin, as the responsible parties.

Khrushchev felt impelled to oppose Beria in this, perhaps out of the need to exercise his growing strength, perhaps to warn the police chief that there were limits to his power. Maneuvering shrewdly among the Kremlin leaders, Khrushchev was able to save Ignatiev; Ryumin, however, was arrested and later executed. He was guilty, it was said, of extracting confessions ". . . by methods which were inadmissible and strictly forbidden by Soviet law."

On April 14, Beria announced the arrest of the Georgian Minister of State Security, Rukhzade. At the same time, victims of the Georgian Plot, concocted in 1952 by Stalin and Ignatiev as a preliminary to the purge of Beria himself, were released.

Here were clear indications of a mounting power struggle inside the Kremlin. Exposés of supposed crimes involving innocent people were designed to implicate many of those guiding the country. Beria was threatening the entire system in his drive for prestige and power, and many members of the apparatus became alarmed.

For Khrushchev, this was proof of an old theory of his— never frighten people unnecessarily; create no enemies, if possible. From his lofty position as Party chief, he continued to publicize the advantages of collective leadership. When he exercised his authority over the Soviet press he was careful that every member of the Presidium received prominent mention, always making certain to assert the principle of Party control over all areas of Soviet life.

Beria meanwhile, linked immutably to his cruel and bloody past, sought desperately to compensate for it. He detected his political salvation in a dramatic liberalization of domestic policy, at the same time making a grand gesture for the support of non-Russian Communist states, then under Moscow's domination. With that in mind, he began to meddle in the affairs of East Germany, urging upon its leaders a course of comparative gentleness.

Khrushchev stood opposed to too much tolerance. Intuition told him that it was a dangerous path to follow. He believed in the historical assertion that rebellions occur not when repression is most intense but when people are allowed wider freedom.

He was right. On June 16, 1953, the people of East Berlin rose up against their Communist leaders. Many people defected to the West, reporting that the East German government had asked for armed assistance from Moscow to help in putting down the rebellion.

Here was a dilemma for the Kremlin. Uncertainty, restlessness and discontent were on the rise throughout the Communist empire, and the virus of rebellion might be contagious. Against this was the logic that insisted that armed intervention and the killing of civilians might bring about even more destructive results.

The rebellion spread throughout the Soviet Zone of divided Germany, erupting in Leipzig, Halle, Magdeburg and in other industrial districts. The worsening situation became intolerable to the men in the Kremlin, including Khrushchev, and they acted. Russian tanks and Russian bayonets routed the rebels and crushed the opposition.

There were some things in the world that the Red Army

could not do, however. It could not, for example, influence the twenty-five thousand North Korean and Chinese prisoners of war who refused to be repatriated at the end of the Korean War, electing to remain under South Korean jurisdiction.

Here was exactly what the Soviet hierarchy had feared when Stalin died—a spread of disorder, of reactions to past suppression. The East Germans, the Chinese, the North Koreans, all were casting a telling vote against Communism. Corrective measures were required, some one was needed to blame for past errors.

Lavrenti Beria was the likeliest candidate. The East Berlin trouble had shocked Malenkov and Molotov so that now they moved in with the anti-Beria majority in the Presidium. Malenkov took a leading role, suggesting to the Central Committee and the Presidium that Beria be arrested and demoted.

Beria was charged with anti-Party, anti-State activity, seeking to ". . . place the Ministry of Internal Affairs above the Government and the Communist Party." Malenkov went further, insisting that Beria had tried to damage the reforms then being attempted.

Khrushchev, as Party chief, made certain that *Pravda* printed his message of Party supremacy in this and any similar affairs:

Only collective political experience, only the collective wisdom of the Central Committee . . . can guarantee the correct leadership of the Party and country, the unshakeable unity and solidarity of the Party ranks, the successful building of Communism. . . . Any official, no matter what post he occupies, must be subject to the unrelaxed supervision of the Party.

Beria learned quickly that he had made enemies not only in the Kremlin but among the generals of the Red Army who resented his emphasis on consumer goods at the expense of the hardware of war. Beria was charged with undermining the friendship of non-Russian people of the Communist camp, of being in the employ of foreigners, of disregarding socialist legality and even of working for British Intelligence.

The fact that there was no firm evidence to support the charges failed to deter those who were against Beria. Khrushchev's version of these events was given to a French visitor to Moscow in 1956.

Very soon after the death of Stalin, we in the Presidium began to get reports of some game which Beria was playing. We began to have him followed and in a few weeks we established the fact that our suspicions were justified. He was clearly preparing a conspiracy against the Presidium. . . . We designated a special session of the Presidium, to which, of course, Beria was invited too. He appeared, apparently not suspecting that we knew anything. And right there we began to cross-question him, to adduce facts, data, to put questions to him, in other words, we put him through a cross-examination which lasted four hours.

For all of us it was clear that he was really guilty, and that this man could be dangerous to the Party and the country.

We left him alone in the room . . . And we went into another room and there had a discussion of what should be done with him.

Our inner conviction of his guilt was unshakeable. But at that time we did not have at our disposal a sufficient amount of juridical evidence of his guilt. And we found ourselves in a difficult position. Evidence for his consignment to a court we still did not have, yet to leave him at liberty was impossible.

We came to the unanimous decision that the only correct

measure for the defense of the revolution was to shoot him immediately. This decision was adopted by us, and carried out on the spot.

But we felt much easier when, some time after his condemnation, we received sufficient and irrefutable evidence of his guilt.

This tack completed, Khrushchev's personal organization men began demoting or removing from office Beria's followers and reversing his policies. During this procedure the man of the Ukraine was careful to alarm no one with his increasing exercise of power.

That he was successful became clear when Khrushchev was named First Secretary of the Central Committee in September, 1953. Beria's death profited Khrushchev even more; formerly ranked fifth in the Soviet hierarchy, he was now listed third, behind Malenkov and Molotov. In fact, however, with the Party apparatus in his strong peasant hands, he was actually the number two man in the country. Though the world at large paid him almost no attention, Khrushchev was very nearly at the same position Joseph Stalin had occupied after Lenin's death.

The parallel would be extended further.

10

A month prior to Khrushchev's appointment as First Secretary another equally important development took place in the Soviet Union—scientists exploded their first hydrogen bomb. Russia had joined the United States as a full-fledged nuclear power. The peoples of the world shuddered and prayed for compassionate leadership and peace.

For Nikita Khrushchev, a rewarding tide flowed in his favor. He studied the changes taking place in the country and, for the most part, approved of what he saw. He had shored up Party weaknesses and felt more secure after the departure of Beria. The new course, with a broad easing of restrictions and a general softening of policy, made good sense and fortified the collective leadership. It made the transition from the one-man rule of Stalin easier, smoother. Still, he had questions. How much freedom was to be allowed the people? and in what areas? Where should the limits on open discussion and criticism be placed? Khrushchev wondered about the satellite countries of Eastern and Central Europe; how would this leniency affect them?

Most important to Khrushchev was the role of the Party in the affairs of the nation. He had made up his mind to one thing: there would be no lessening of Party influence, no diminishment of Party authority—*his* authority.

A division of power between Government and Party had never arisen before because Stalin ruled both with an iron grip.

But things were different now, and Khrushchev was determined to maintain Party preeminence in all matters.

There was considerable ferment in intellectual and artistic areas against official meddling. Author A. Salinsky wrote in October, 1953:

> The saddest thing is that some of the writers have not freed themselves from the internal censor who for so long sat at the side of the writer and bound his thought, his tongue.

And the following month, a young critic, V. Pomerantisev, said:

> Do not think about prosecution. Don't feel compelled to set down your conclusions, remain silent if necessary, but don't let yourself write a single line that you do not feel. Be independent.

And the world-famous composer, Khachaturian said:

> I think it is high time an end was put to the present system of administrative guardianship over composers . . . Let every composer do his work on his own responsibility . . . no more "directives" from our bureaucrats . . .

Changes continued to be made. Malenkov announced his New Course, placing food and light industries on a plane equal with heavy industry.

Seeing the direction in which Malenkov was moving, and convinced that he could make this a battleground to advance his own political cause, Khrushchev delivered a speech on agriculture, about which he was considered an expert. He came out for things people could understand and which they approved; a simplification of governmental bureaucracy, the transfer of

110

excess officials into the countryside, a demand for more cows and permission for each peasant to own privately one or two cows.

Such speeches were not enough for the new First Secretary, and he worked his will in many areas hidden from public view. He fired Vasily Andrianov, Secretary of the Leningrad Party and a Malenkov supporter. He set about changing the leadership in Armenia. These Beria-men were replaced by Khrushchev's friends. He was determined to transform the Party into a personal power base and continued to work to this end.

His reasoning was simple. The nation was beginning to enjoy its new freedom. Men were talking about a variety of subjects ranging from farming to literature, from industrialization to political ideology. They even discussed the possibility that everything Western wasn't evil and destructive. As a result, the Party was becoming more and more important, the source of ultimate truth and guidance. Khrushchev was fast becoming the Party.

It was easier to argue such matters than it was to grow grain enough to feed all the people of Russia. At this point, Khrushchev made a move designed to elevate his stature even further, to make a concrete contribution to the national good. He offered a carefully prepared plan, proposing that agricultural emphasis be placed on the development of a whole new region, one that had never before been under cultivation—the Virgin Lands of the Volga Region, Siberia, the Ural Mountains area and Northern Kazakhstan.

It was a simple idea: great numbers of workers and technicians were to be moved into the designated Virgin Lands, along with an immense allocation of the necessary machinery; 250,000 volunteers, 120,000 tractors and 10,000 harvesters. Thirty-two million acres were to be developed, more than three times the amount of land currently under the plow.

Khrushchev expected to hear prophecies of disaster and he did. It was claimed the regions involved would become wastelands, that nothing good would result, that the scheme would sabotage Malenkov's consumer goods policy. The last prediction was accurate. Industry that otherwise would have turned out automobiles and refrigerators, toasters and washing machines, was turned to making farm implements and equipment.

In support of the Virgin Lands, Khrushchev began to make his authority be known. He criticized government bureaus for obstructionism, for failing to provide the required manpower and materials, for lack of imagination, daring and will. He apportioned blame for all setbacks while accepting whatever credit was to be gained for himself.

Malenkov had every reason to expect the Virgin Lands plan to bring about Khrushchev's downfall. Anything so grand in scope and so ambitious in concept would be certain to run into massive problems, many of which would be impossible to overcome. Moreover, Malenkov was in a position to subvert the plan each step of the way and in this he could depend upon the assistance of Molotov and Kaganovich. His other senior ministers, Mikoyan and Bulganin, would provide neutrality and neutrality would work in his favor.

But he failed to reckon with Khrushchev's sharp understanding of Soviet internal politics. The First Secretary wasted no time in attacking, announcing hotly that the new agricultural policies would ". . . meet with stubborn resistance from the bureaucrats."

Malenkov found himself on the defensive. To emphasize the production of consumer goods was good, but not when it was at the expense of what was considered Communist dogma, the development of heavy industry. Not even the members of the Old Guard would support such heresy. Yet, Russia was economically unable to maintain a high level of production in both fields, despite the cut in the military budget at the close of the Korean War.

Malenkov was determined to go further, however. With both the Soviet Union and the United States in possession of nuclear weapons, there seemed to be mutual deterrence to war between

Khrushchev speaks in Kazakhstan as part of his virgin-soil campaign.

the two great powers. This led Malenkov into making a statement that a nuclear war would destroy capitalism *and* Communism as well. Never before had a Russian leader dared question the declarations of Marx and Lenin that Communism was invincible.

Khrushchev attacked. He stressed the supremacy of Soviet nuclear power and insisted that any agreement with the capitalist world, and especially the United States, was nearly impossible.

So politically untenable was Malenkov's position that his words were eventually reversed to read that war would signify ". . . the end of the Western world, but not of Communism."

Khrushchev maintained pressure on Malenkov at all fronts. His Party cadres, groups of skilled agitators working across the countryside, refused to lend support to Malenkov's ideas. Since terror was no longer a primary weapon in executing policy, propaganda and manpower had become increasingly important. Khrushchev knew how to wield both and had spent many long hours over the years developing a personal apparatus that would respond to his wishes. A barrage of propaganda was unloosed in behalf of his Virgin Lands scheme. He managed to bully into being a declaration calling for its acceleration, signed by both the Party and the Government. Significantly, the Party imprint came first this time, an upgrading that was noted by officials large and small. They understood that a new strong man was emerging out of the ranks.

Determined to expand his influence, his reputation and his awareness of foreign affairs, Khrushchev embarked on a journey to China with Bulganin and Mikoyan. The Minister of Foreign Affairs, Molotov, was not included in the group, a notable omission arranged, many people thought, by the First Secretary of the Party for his own advantage.

It did seem that way. In Peking, Khrushchev attended the celebration of the fifth anniversary of the Communist regime in China, thus setting himself up as the official representative of the USSR. Not satisfied, he made a bold move, concluding a trade arrangement with Mao Tse-tung, China's leader, which would furnish that country with complete factories, as well as other heavy industry. This meant that Russia would be forced to increase its own heavy industry in order to fulfill the obligation, all against Malenkov's designs.

The journey also provided Khrushchev with a chance to mend his political relationships with Mikoyan and Bulganin. At the conclusion of the Oriental visit it was clear that Khrushchev had developed his reputation in foreign affairs, had made himself Mao Tse-tung's favorite in the Kremlin and had developed a pair of key friends in Malenkov's own camp.

Khrushchev didn't wait long before using his new strength. A few days after his return, he issued a policy directive concerned with religion. Comparatively unimportant itself, the directive was signed by only Khrushchev, not by the Presidium of the Central Committee. By setting such a precedent, the peasant strong boy was taking more power into his hands.

Khrushchev continued on the offensive, growing bolder each time. He grew critical of Stalinist *methods,* but not of his *aims,* and attacked officials who still practiced those methods. It was no coincidence that some of these turned out to be friends and colleagues of Malenkov. One was Victor Abakumov, Minister of State Security. He, along with five of his subordinates, was charged with crimes committed in 1949 in Leningrad, convicted and executed.

Here was a blow that hurt Malenkov badly for it showed that he could not protect his supporters. Furthermore, it linked him with the terrible past, with the awful practices of Stalin and Beria.

Khrushchev pushed forward with unceasing energy, exploiting every opportunity that came his way. At a rally of young people, he issued an edict which changed the date of the holiday honoring Lenin. No one dared object for Khrushchev had simply transferred the celebration from the day of Lenin's death to the day of his birth.

In January, 1955, Khrushchev, confident because he had the backing of the Party, the secret police and the Red Army, delivered a powerful attack before the Central Committee, utilizing the brutal verbal style of Stalin's era. He declared:

> In connection with the measures lately taken for increasing the output of consumer goods, some comrades have confused the question of the pace of development of heavy and light industry in our country . . . These pseudo-theoreticians try to claim that at some stage of socialist construction the development of heavy industry ceases to be the main task and that light industry can and should overtake all other branches of industry. This is profoundly incorrect reasoning, alien to the spirit of Marxism-Leninism —nothing but slander of our Party. This is a belching up of the Rightist Deviation, a regurgitation of views hostile to Leninism . . .

Who were the "some comrades" mentioned, the "pseudo-theoreticians," the "slanderers of the Party"? Most of Khrushchev's listeners thought they knew. Back in August, 1953, Malenkov had said: "We can and therefore must, in the interest of securing a more rapid rise in the material and cultural standard of living of the people, force the development of light industry by all means."

Malenkov sensed the winds of change were blowing him out of office. Little time remained to him and he knew it. He meant to salvage what was left to him. On February 8, in the great Kremlin hall, with all members of the Presidium on the platform, the Supreme Soviet convened. Thirteen hundred delegates listened in stunned silence while the Chairman of the Supreme Soviet read a statement prepared by Comrade Malenkov in which he asked for permission to resign, to be replaced ". . . by another Comrade with greater administrative experience . . . I recognize clearly that my insufficient experience in local work has an unfavorable effect on the fulfillment of the complicated and responsible duties of the Chairman of Council of Ministers, as well as the fact that I have not had the opportunity of being directly responsible for individual branches of the economy in another ministry or in any other economic body." He went on to confess his ". . . guilt and responsibility for the unsatisfactory state of affairs in agriculture . . ." and praised Khrushchev's reforms, saying that they were ". . . based upon the only correct foundation—the further all-round development of heavy industry—and only the realization of this program will provide the necessary conditions for a real increase in the production of all necessary consumers' goods."

Here was a dramatic reversal, an admission not only of failure but of the correctness of his opponent's position in all things. Malenkov was fortunate in his timing. Had this been the Stalin era he would have been forced to confess to more insidious crimes, admit to being an agent of the imperialists and an enemy of the people. Now, however, instead of being shot, he was merely demoted to Minister of Power Stations and Deputy Chairman of the Council of Ministers.

Having just witnessed the humbling of his primary opponent, and at the same time displayed the new Soviet justice and humanity to the world, Khrushchev took center stage himself, rising to nominate a replacement for Malenkov.

". . . In the name of the Central Committee of the Communist Party of the Soviet Union," he intoned, offering a ". . . true son of the Communist Party, the servant of the Soviet people, the worthy pupil of the great Lenin, the close colleague of Lenin's successor, J. V. Stalin, the excellent Party and State functionary, the First Deputy Prime Minister and Minister of Defense of the U.S.S.R., Nikolai Alexandrovich Bulganin . . ."

Bulganin was a former supporter of Malenkov, a friend easily won and just as easily directed and controlled by a determined Party chieftain. This was a characteristic move, salving the bruised egos of Khrushchev's opponents even as he won a massive victory.

The nomination was approved by acclamation. Nikita Sergeyevich, the peasant from the Donets mines, Hero of Stalingrad, Defender of Collective Leadership, Farming Expert, World Traveller, Chief of the Communist Party, Man of the People, had just named the Prime Minister of the Union of Soviet Socialist Republics.

11

At age sixty-one, Khrushchev was vitally active. The years of struggle and strain had done nothing to lessen his ambition for himself and for Mother Russia. Though he was now the most powerful man in the country, he was still relatively unknown outside the Soviet Union. More important, he was aware that the autocracy of Stalin was dead and buried, and that the collective leadership could, and at any time might, yank him off his high perch.

An article in *Pravda* pointed this up:

Lenin taught us the collective nature of work. He often reminded us that all members of the Politburo are equal and that the secretary is chosen to execute the resolutions of the Central Committee of the Party.

Here was a reminder to Khrushchev that Malenkov, still a member of the Politburo and the Presidium, even then had considerable personal influence and remained a very real threat. Thus, the First Secretary decided to spend a considerable portion of 1955 consolidating his position and fortifying himself for the struggles he sensed lay ahead. As part of this effort, he went abroad three times during the year, accompanied by Bulganin.

First, they went to Yugoslavia. When that country's ruler, Marshal Tito, had refused to take orders from Moscow, Stalin had excommunicated Yugoslavia from the True Society of Communism. But now, with the USSR seeking to expand its influence and infiltrate its ideology throughout Europe, a recalcitrant Communist country was an unwanted obstacle. On a pragmatic basis, eastern Europe was a defensive barrier for Russia, and Yugoslavia was a vulnerable chink.

As soon as he stepped off his plane in Belgrade, Khrushchev acted to correct Stalin's error and promptly committed one of his own. He said:

> We sincerely regret what has occurred and are determinedly removing all those obstacles which have accumulated during this period. In this, we, for our part, must include the provocative role played in the relations between Yugoslavia and the USSR by the enemies of the people, Beria, Abakumov, and others, who have now been unmasked. We have carefully examined the material upon which those grave accusations and insults aimed then at the Yugoslav leaders were based. The facts have shown that this material was concocted by enemies of the people, despicable agents of imperialism who had joined the ranks of our Party by underhand means.

This was familiar double-talk to Marshal Tito, no different than he had listened to many times from Russian leaders. Khrushchev was supposed to be rectifying Stalin's errors but was using the same kind of language the "Man of Steel" had so often used. Tito's guard stayed high.

Despite this antipathy, the meetings produced a statement that shook the Communist alliance, as well as the Western world, a statement that came to be known as the Belgrade Declaration. Its key provision stated that ". . . Differences in practical forms of socialism are exclusively the affairs of individual countries" and that these countries were entitled to ". . . walk different roads toward socialism."

Here was a revolutionary departure from traditional Communist thought which held that only a single avenue to utopia existed, Moscow's way. This was only one step in Khrushchev's break with the past. On his way home, he stopped in Sofia, Bulgaria. There, in secret party conclave, he made his first attack on the person and the policies of Joseph Stalin, the preface for more meaningful changes to come, more dramatic pronouncements.

Upon his return to Moscow, Khrushchev discovered that Molotov was opposed to the Belgrade Declaration, holding to the old, hard line against Tito. Khrushchev reacted like an angry bear, hitting out with every weapon he owned, attacking Molotov politically and personally. The onslaught was too much for Molotov; and he finally put his name to a statement declaring that, in the future, he would support all policies of the Central Committee, policies which in fact were those of Nikita Sergeyevich.

Seven days later, Khrushchev traveled to Geneva, Switzerland, to attend a summit meeting with such world leaders as President Eisenhower, England's Prime Minister Anthony Eden and Premier Fauré of France. Flanking him at this confrontation were Molotov, not yet exposed to *public* humiliation, Bulganin and Marshal Zhukov.

Khrushchev sat quietly during most of the conference, assessing the Western leadership and seeking to understand them, to learn their personal strengths and their weaknesses. He moved about on his own, without bodyguards, a man among men, talking easily, listening, watching, learning.

As former comrades-in-arms during World War II, Marshal Zhukov had a long talk with President Eisenhower and the latter's reactions were reported in *The New York Times:*

> The President revealed . . . that the Soviet Minister of Defense had offered him a firsthand account of what had been going on within the inner barriers of the Iron Curtain . . . He implied that it had been a persuasive account, particularly in the stress it laid on collective leadership . . . General Eisenhower said the new system had been

demonstrated in the working conditions at Geneva, where he had noted that the Soviet representatives conferred constantly and produced a common viewpoint . . .

What Eisenhower could not know was that Marshal Zhukov had been brought back from military oblivion by Khrushchev, whom he respected and trusted, and that Khrushchev was now actively backing the Red Army in its budgetary demands and in its emphasis on heavy industry. Nor did the President understand that Bulganin was a man of limited intellectual means, malleable and almost totally subservient to the muscular little man in the poor-fitting clothes who sat silently for the most part, his bullet-head sunk between powerful shoulders. Nor could the President know that only a week before Khrushchev had delivered a political mauling to Molotov which forced the old Bolshevik to do his bidding.

Though little of value came of that summit meeting, Khrushchev realized that having Molotov there had restored some of his prestige. It was a situation easily corrected. Back on February 8, the day Malenkov had resigned from the premiership, Molotov had uttered these words: "In the Soviet Union where the foundations of the socialist society have already been built . . ." The *foundations* of the socialist society? What more telling and self-incriminating remark could be made? To even suggest that Socialism was less than fully realized in the USSR was to contradict Communist dogma.

Khrushchev leaped viciously upon the error seven months after the fact. It was a shaken Molotov who was forced into a public recantation of his views, admitting that he had underestimated the advances of Socialism and that he had failed to recognize the advanced stage to which Communism had come.

The job was done. To all practical purposes, Molotov was finished, as were Malenkov and Beria. In one way or another, Khrushchev had eliminated each of his enemies and had forged ahead of them in the political hierarchy.

Native dancers on the island of Bali greet Khrushchev.

There was more to be done. A cadre of veterans of Stalin's era still existed in the State Security System of Georgia. Khrushchev got rid of them with characteristic efficiency. This done, he "rehabilitated" Stalin's victims; most of them were long dead, however, and so took no joy in this event.

Trying to overlook nothing in his drive for power, Khrushchev ridiculed the expensive and ornate architecture and decoration in public places, such as the Moscow subway, the result of so much work on his part. The irony of this apparently escaped his attention. At the same time, he voiced his displeasure with the growing liberal attitudes of the intellectuals and demanded that writers, poets, composers and artists get in line with the ". . . spirit of the new . . ."

Nor did he neglect his primary province, the Party. During one period in 1955, nine thousand Party secretaries in the Ukraine and twenty-five hundred more in Georgia were replaced with Khrushchev's men.

Now that Molotov was out of the way, Khrushchev felt secure enough to leave the country again, to further fortify his reputation in foreign affairs. With Bulganin in tow, leading the world to believe they were equals in authority, he embarked on a long tour of India, Burma and Afghanistan.

To insure the success of this expedition, it was necessary to make another strategic withdrawal from the orthodoxy of Stalinism. Hundreds of ideological publications and textbooks had to be disowned, rewritten or withdrawn completely from use so as not to give offense in the countries he was to visit. An entire edition of the *Bolshava Sovietskaya Encyclopedia* was destroyed and rewritten in accord with the "different roads to socialism" concept. Many other ancient dogmas had to be revised.

At the same time, Khrushchev wanted to keep the Stalinists happy. While in Mandalay, he said: "The colonizers who lorded it in your country retarded your development. We Europeans feel ashamed for these Europeans who oppressed you, who plundered you. Yet, not all Europeans think and act as coloniz-ers who consider that their white skin gives them the right to dominate those with black skins."

Not satisfied, he unloosed another diatribe two days later, blaming the United States, England and France for helping "the Hitlerite bloodhound to be set against Russia." Conveni-ently, he forgot the Hitler-Stalin non-aggression pact and the role played by the Allies in World War II.

Wherever he went, Khrushchev appealed to the nationalistic and religious sentiments of the people, promising aid without any strings attached. He went so far as to wear a hat like that worn by the Indian leader Mahatma Gandhi, though Soviet propaganda claimed that Gandhi was a ". . . petty bourgeois demagogue who misled the people by exploiting their backward, religious feelings." In his own way, Nikita Sergeyevich sought to make friends and win converts.

As 1956 came into being, Khrushchev claimed a unique position in Russia. Among equals in the Politburo, he was somehow more equal than the others. More outgoing than most and able to reach the people, he possessed many of the qualities of a Western politician. Deeply patriotic, he was not above manipulating the people when it seemed necessary, seeing them as a faceless mass. Yet he was happiest among them, still the peasant, raucous and jovial, free with advice on how to plant potatoes and milk cows.

He feared the West, especially the United States, seeing her as the new Imperial Power. He feared the rearming of West Germany and opposed the reunification of that land, remem-bering clearly the rape and murder committed by the Nazis in Russia, a face the Germans had been careful not to show the Western Allies.

But he recognized also the need for change and he insisted that war between Socialism and capitalism was no longer "fatally inevitable"; he realized now that Malenkov had been right after all, that nuclear war would destroy both systems.

125

Studying the Communist camp, he anticipated no difficulty with his European satellites. They were, after all, Russian domains run by local officials who were easily controlled. As for China, Mao Tse-tung was no puppet, but Khrushchev intended to tighten the bonds between the two countries, no matter how difficult it might be.

He was optimistic about the future. As conditions warranted it, he would advance the cause of World Revolution. At the same time, he expected to be able to forestall any more defections, such as Marshal Tito's.

It was his intention to show the world that Russia was a peaceful giant, endangered by warlike imperialism on all fronts, but equipped to defend herself and her friends. With this in mind, Khrushchev was prepared to deal with any nation, no matter how anti-Communist it might be. India was an example of this as was Egypt, where the Communist Party had been declared illegal.

To accomplish all this in the climate of independence and freedom then abroad in the world, the Soviet Union had to cast off all the remaining inhibitory bonds of Stalin and Stalinism. Khrushchev's speech in Sofia had been a first step in this direction and he had been carefully laying the groundwork for additional steps.

Some members of the Politburo would oppose any radical move away from the past. For a quarter of a century they had lived and profited from Stalin's terror, corruption and lies and had encouraged the people to worship the "Man of Steel" as a deity. For them, the truth was an enemy to be feared and suppressed.

Khrushchev thought otherwise. To him, the time had come to unearth the evils of the past. The time had come to shake off the remaining strictures of Stalinism, to assert himself and to take the reins of power into his own big fists. It was Nikita Sergeyevich's time, and he knew it.

12

The Twentieth Congress of the Communist Party of the Soviet Union convened in the Great Hall of the Kremlin Palace on February 14, 1956, before fifteen hundred delegates plus many more fraternal delegates. Khrushchev rose to welcome them and was met by tempestuous and prolonged applause. It held and increased, an ovation that far outstripped anything accorded other Kremlin leaders.

When at last the delegates quieted and settled back in their seats, Khrushchev began to talk, a long speech in which he made a concession to the supporters of Stalinism, speaking of Stalin's death as a loss to Communism. But, he also set the stage for what was to come as he linked Stalin with Gottwald of Czechoslovakia and Japan's Tokuda, relatively unimportant figures in the Socialist camp. He recalled:

Shortly after the Nineteenth Congress of the Party death took Joseph Vissarionovich Stalin from our ranks. The enemies of socialism counted on the possibility of confusion in the ranks of our Party, of discord in its leadership . . . These calculations came to nought . . . The unity of our Party has been built up over the years and decades; it grew and was strengthened in the struggle with a multiplicity of enemies. Trotskyists, Bukharinists, bourgeois nationalists and other vicious enemies of the people . . .

Enemies of the people . . . That infamous phrase came out

of the Great Terror, and it alerted his listeners that something vital to them all was imminent. They were right, and before many days had passed Khrushchev would again use that odious set of words, but in another context, in his secret denunciation of Stalin. Then he said:

> Stalin originated the concept "enemy of the people." This term automatically rendered it unnecessary that the ideological errors of a man or men engaged in a controversy be proven: this term made possible the usage of the most cruel repression, violating all norms of revolutionary legality, against anyone who in any way disagreed with Stalin, against those who were only suspected of hostile intent, against those who had bad reputations. This concept "enemy of the people," actually eliminated the possibility of any kind of ideological fight or the making of one's views known on this or that issue, even those of a practical character . . .
>
> This led to glaring violations of revolutionary legality, and to the fact that many entirely innocent persons, who in the past had defended the Party line, became victims. We must assert that in regard to those persons who in their time had opposed the Party line, there were often no sufficiently serious reasons for their physical annihilation. The formula "enemy of the people" was specifically introduced for the purpose of physically annihilating such individuals.

The shock of Khrushchev's attack on Soviet Russia's former master, had been softened somewhat by earlier speeches by Mikoyan and Suslov, both criticizing Stalin. These, though extreme enough in content, were mild in tone. The declarations of Nikita Sergeyevich were not. His words were carefully chosen and carefully arranged, larded with self-righteousness and the violence of denunciation. It was his purpose to shred the memory of the man he had once supported loyally in all things.

It is clear that in a whole series of cases, Stalin showed his intolerance, his brutality, and his abuse of power. Instead of proving that he was right and thus gaining the support of the masses, he often chose the path of repression and physical annihilation, not only of actual enemies, but also of individuals who had not committed any crimes against the Party and the Soviet government. Here we see no wisdom but only a demonstration of that brutal force that had once so alarmed V. I. Lenin.

Khrushchev had no intention of making the same mistake; he intended to cite chapter and verse in mauling the reputation of the dead dictator. One way to do it was by reviving the cruel and bloody activities of Stalin's equally dead supporter, the notorious chief of the Secret Police, Lavrenti Beria.

"An example of vile provocation," Khrushchev recalled with dismay in his voice, "of odious falsification, and of criminal violation of revolutionary legality is the case of Comrade Eikhe, a Party member since 1905." He offered a litany of persecution and torture to which Eikhe had been subjected. The account ended abruptly: "On February 4, Eikhe was shot."

Some of the delegates stirred uneasily, and with reason. Like Khrushchev himself, they too had been privy to what had been happening during the Great Purge. Some of them had actually taken part in terrible activities which they would have preferred to forget, and have others do likewise. But Comrade Khrushchev had much more to say on the subject.

I wish to recall Beria's bestial disposition of the cases of Kedrov, Golubiev, and Golubiev's adopted mother, Baturina—persons who wished to inform the Central Committee concerning Beria's treacherous activity. They were shot without any trial, and the sentence was passed *ex post facto,* after the execution. Here is what the old Communist Comrade Kerov wrote to the Central Committee:

I am calling to you for help from a gloomy cell of the Lefortorsky prison. Let my cry of horror reach your ears . . .

I suffer innocently . . . I am an old Bolshevik free of any stain; I have honestly fought for almost forty years in the ranks of the Party for the good and the prosperity of the nation . . .

. . . Today I, a sixty-two-year-old man, am being threatened by the investigating judges with severe, cruel, and degrading methods of physical pressure. . . .

But I have no way out. I cannot ward off the new and rapidly approaching powerful blows.

. . . My health is broken, my strength and my energy are waning, the end is drawing near. To die in a Soviet prison, branded as a vile traitor to the Motherland— what can be more monstrous for an honest old man? . . . Neither the Party, nor the Soviet government, nor the people's commissar, L. P. Beria, will permit this cruel, irreparable injustice . . . I believe deeply that truth and justice will triumph. I believe. I believe.

Such examples went far to condemn Stalin and Beria, but since Khrushchev had been a member of the apparatus for so long, some people might logically associate him with the terror of those awful days. Too shrewd to let that happen, he took care to display his "bloodless" hands to the Congress, stressing Stalin's unilateral decisions.

I can remember how the Ukraine learned about Kossior's arrest. The Kiev Radio used to start its broadcast thus: "This is Radio Kossior." When one day the broadcast began without naming Kossior, everyone was quite certain that something had happened to Kossior, that he had probably been arrested.

In case any of those in the hall failed to understand, he explained further:

We are justly accusing Yezhov for the degenerate practices of 1937. But we have to answer these questions: Could Yezhov have arrested Kossior, for instance, without the knowledge of Stalin? Was there an exchange of opinions or a Political Bureau decision concerning this? No, there was not, as there was none regarding other cases of this type. Could Yezhov have decided such important matters as the fate of such eminent Party figures? No, it would be a display of naïveté to consider this the work of Yezhov alone. It is clear that these matters were decided by Stalin, and that without his orders and his sanction Yezhov could not have done this.

It is clear that these matters were decided by Stalin . . . There was no doubt about Khrushchev's meaning. *He* had reached this conclusion after assessing the available evidence and he expected his listeners to do likewise.

We have examined the cases of, and have rehabilitated Kossior, Rudzutak, Postyshev, Kosaryev, and others. For what causes were they arrested and sentenced? The review of evidence shows that there was no reason for this . . . In such a situation there is no need for any sanction, for what sort of a sanction could there be when Stalin decided everything?

Stalin decided everything . . . Perhaps. But Khrushchev failed to mention that when Kossior fell it was to a three-man purge team sent by Stalin to the Ukraine, a team composed of Molotov, Yezhov and Nikita Sergeyevich Khrushchev.

As he attacked and downgraded Stalin, Khrushchev very smartly justified and defended his own past, at the same time

131

placing a protective blanket over some of those who had supported him along the way. There was, for example, Ignatiev,
the former chief of Security Police, under whose rule the doctors' plot had been invented and executed. Khrushchev intended
to absolve him of all guilt in the matter.

> Present at this Congress is the former Minister of State
> Security, Comrade Ignatiev. Stalin told him curtly: "If you
> don't obtain confessions from the doctors, we will shorten
> you by a head."

Khrushchev spoke on, forgiving with a high degree of selec-
tivity, justifying the actions of his followers and condemning
those who had opposed him, those who still remained a threat
to his ambition. That all members of the apparatus had functioned under Stalin's orders, that no one, including himself,
had dared oppose the "Man of Steel," was conveniently ignored
or rationalized.

There was one more penetrating condemnation of Stalin and
his rule to be made, made in the light of the new collective
leadership and made, too, because of Khrushchev's personal
aspirations. The cult of personality and its inevitable result,
mass repressions, had to be disowned.

> What is the reason that mass repression against activists
> increased more and more after the Seventeenth Party Con-
> gress? It was because at that time Stalin had so elevated
> himself above the Party and above the nation that he
> ceased to consider either the Central Committee or the
> Party . . .

Khrushchev blustered on in that vigorous and overbearing
way so familiar to his associates:

> If, today we sharply criticize the cult of personality which
> was so widespread during Stalin's life, and if we speak

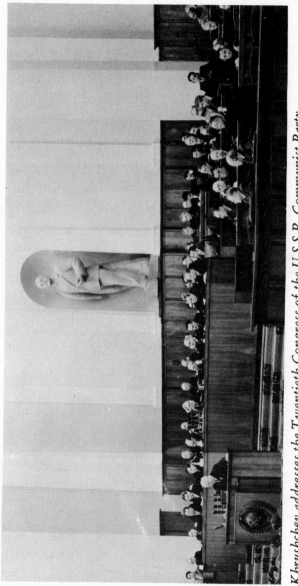

Khrushchev addresses the Twentieth Congress of the U.S.S.R. Communist Party.

about the many negative phenomena generated by this cult, alien to the spirit of Marxism-Leninism, some people might ask: "How could it be? Stalin headed the party and the country for thirty years, and many victories were won during his lifetime. Can we deny this?" . . . In my opinion the question can be asked in this manner only by those who are blinded and hopelessly hypnotized by the cult of personality, only by those who do not understand the essence of the Revolution and of the Soviet state, only by those who do not understand, in a Leninist manner, the role of the Party and of the people in the development of Soviet society.

With those words Khrushchev made clear that whoever dared question his interpretation of what had passed understood nothing about the Communist Revolution and so stood perched on the edge of some undefined criminal action and its implied punishment.

At last he came to the conclusion of the lengthy secret speech, still anxious to reduce Stalin's memory to more manageable proportions, at the same time limiting his own thrust for power and beginning a new era for the Soviet Union.

Comrades! We must abolish the cult of personality decisively, once and for all; we must draw the proper conclusions concerning both ideological-theoretical and practical work.

It is necessary for this purpose:

First, in a Bolshevik manner, to condemn and to eradicate the cult of personality as alien to Marxism-Leninism . . .

. . . We will be forced to do much work in order to examine . . . and to correct the widespread erroneous views connected with the cult of personality in the sphere of history, philosophy, economy, and of other sciences, as well as in literature and the fine arts. It is especially necessary that in the immediate future we compile a serious textbook of the history of our party which will be edited with scientific Marxist objectivity, a textbook of the history of Soviet society, a book pertaining to the events of the civil war and the great patriotic war.

Secondly to continue . . . the work done by the Party's Central Committee during the last years, a work characterized, above all, by the main principle of collective leadership.

Thirdly, to restore completely the Leninist principles of Soviet Socialist democracy, expressed in the Constitution of the Soviet Union, to fight the willfulness of individuals abusing their power. The evil caused by acts violating revolutionary Socialist legality which have accumulated during a long time as a result of the negative influence of the cult of the individual has to be completely corrected.

When Khrushchev finished speaking, two things were clear to his listeners: the deification of Joseph Stalin had been shattered, and the peasant boy of Kalinovka stood at the summit of the Soviet Union, the most powerful man in the country.

There was a new vocabulary in the USSR, a language that required interpretation and understanding. Many students of Communism seemed to think that Russia had made a formal renunciation of her role as the leader in violent revolution and as the destroyer of the capitalist world.

Others rejected this conclusion and insisted that everything that was happening was little more than political propaganda, designed to advance the socialist cause by deceiving its enemies, deception cut in the old Stalin-mold.

They were wrong, as subsequent events bore out. For this was a time of change in Russia, and Khrushchev was the man to bring about those changes, a man right for the transition that was needed and desired in the country.

There were also some people who concluded that Khrushchev had spoken out spontaneously trying to benefit himself by leaping aboard the anti-Stalin bandwagon triggered by Mikoyan. The facts give lie to such conclusions.

The secret speech ran for more than twenty thousand words and was structured with precise calculation, the material included and that omitted arranged to show that from 1934 onward Stalin was an enemy of the Communist Party.

Stalin was denounced for the torture and murder of many men, men who had earlier tortured and killed on his behalf, at his orders. But Khrushchev had not condemned Stalin for any actions taken against Trotsky, Bukharin or their followers, who were still considered enemies of the state and so possessing a very real value to a potentially strong political chief. Nor did Khrushchev criticize any extremes of collectivization, schemes which had failed to produce the desired results on the farms or in the factories. Much of the terror turned loose by Stalin was ignored, though the Army purge of 1937 received mention, a strategic concession to the generals to insure their continued loyalty.

When news of the secret speech became known, it was rumored that Khrushchev had been forced to make it by his colleagues. That, too, made little sense. When, back in June of the previous year, at Sofia, he had ticked off Stalin's errors to the Bulgarians, he had shown himself to be the pacesetter in Russia, a man to be followed and obeyed.

Surely the delivered version of the speech was a compromise, acceptable to the anti-Stalinists as well as those still loyal to the dictator's memory. Clever wording managed to connect Malenkov, Molotov, Voroshilov and Kaganovich with past "mistakes" and left no doubt that Khrushchev was doing exactly what he wanted to do, saying precisely what he wanted to say. Since Mikoyan had actively supported him in this, Khrushchev repaid him by highlighting his anti-Stalinism, displaying him as a brave and wise comrade.

136

Eventually Molotov and Voroshilov were allowed to pose as intended targets of Stalin's enmity, removing the taint of evil from them, but leaving Kaganovich to stand almost alone as a Stalinist.

The immediate result of all this was to Khrushchev's benefit. With the secret speech, he had by-passed, for the moment, at least, collective leadership, moving past the Central Committee, past the Party itself.

News of the secret speech leaked out, inevitably, and there was turmoil within the Soviet Union and in the world beyond the Iron Curtain as well. Few people understood what was happening, and there was considerable speculation about what it all meant.

In time, at Party meetings across the USSR, the speech was read to the faithful and its provisions discussed and argued. Later, the State Department of the United States issued a version which had come into its hands.

Despite the unrest and uncertainty and despite the obvious changes in official Soviet attitudes, the voting makeup of the Presidium remained constant, and it was apparent that Khrushchev's strength rested on a rather finely balanced amalgamation of forces. It was apparent, too, that Khrushchev was not going to be able to rule as Stalin had ruled, having destroyed that possibility himself by painting the nation as greater and more important than any single man in it. As time passed, Khrushchev came to understand that he was as much a prisoner of circumstances as lesser mortals and he chafed under their restrictions. Trouble was inevitable, and, when it came, it would carry the world to the brink of destruction.

13

The name Nikita Sergeyevich Khrushchev was on lips throughout the Communist world, accompanied by concern and questions. Stalinism had been the catechism of Communism, a guideline for nations and men. Now, with a single blunt stroke, people had been told that it had all been a mistake, a cruel error on which they had built their lives.

Teachers wondered what to teach; Stalin was involved in every subject since he had been acclaimed as "humanity's greatest genius." Books were fat with his words, swollen with paeans to his magnificence. They would all have to be replaced, history rewritten, encyclopedias discarded.

Political agitators working among the peasants wondered what they were to agitate for. And against? What should parents tell their children? What should be done about the cities named after Stalin and the millions of portraits of him posted all over the land? How far did the de-Stalinization process go?

Literature, politics, science, labor, wages, freedom of speech, medicine; no corner of Soviet existence was left untouched. Decisions had to be made but there was no program, and finally it was announced that considerable critical meditation was in order to correct the mistakes of the past. "Leninist Soviet Socialist democracy" had to be restored.

Some steps were taken. Pregnant women were awarded extended maternity leaves from their jobs. A law that suspended workers for six months if they were as such as twenty minutes late for work was repealed. Juveniles were permitted to work fewer hours than adults. Members of farming communes, it was decided, were entitled to a certain amount of payment. Studies were launched to improve judicial procedures. The Saturday work period was reduced to six hours.

Other changes took place. Molotov, long the Foreign Minister, was dismissed and replaced by a favorite of Khrushchev's. Kaganovich, the man who had nursed Khrushchev's career over the years, the man instrumental in bringing him to Moscow and in restoring him to a high place in the Ukraine, his mentor and friend, but a firm Stalinist, was fired as chairman of the key Committee on Labor and Wages. Both men were able to retain their membership in the Party Presidium, that so-important source of policy.

Another message was understood by people behind the Iron Curtain: a further relaxation of controls was in order and there would be greater political toleration and freedom. As if to underscore this conclusion, Khrushchev signed an extension of the Belgrade Declaration with Marshal Tito.

There were stirrings throughout the satellites, too. Once suppressed "freedom-writings" were translated and copies distributed. Strikes—illegal in the Communist world—erupted. There was a workers' riot in the Polish city of Poznan, students demonstrated and political differences were aired and debated openly. More and more persons were rehabilitated and workers who had been fired unjustly were allowed to return to their jobs.

People cried out for freedom in what were essentially police states, for national independence and for free speech. A Polish poetess Anna Kamienska referred to all this as ". . . a delirium of impossible possibilities." In Poland, discontent intensified and there were demands that Wladislaw Gomulka, an idealistic Communist who had helped organize the Polish underground against the Germans, be reinstated to his position of leadership. Gomulka had been arrested in 1951 by Stalin because of his ardent national sentiments.

Sensitive to the worsening Polish situation, Khrushchev hurried to Warsaw. He met with the Polish Politburo and promptly lost his peasant temper.

"We have shed our blood to free Poland," he bellowed, "and now you wish to turn it over to the Americans. But you will not succeed! This will not happen!"

He looked at Gomulka standing nearby, antagonism etched into his features. "And who is that?" Khrushchev demanded of the Soviet Ambassador.

Gomulka spoke for himself. "I am Gomulka, whom you kept in jail for three years."

How much this exchange affected Khrushchev is debatable, but at the next session of the Politburo, he had a change of heart, becoming affable and friendly. He stressed the reluctance of the Soviet Party to inject itself into Polish affairs. Why did he change? Perhaps because of Soviet Marshal Rokossovsky, a man of Polish origins, who informed Khrushchev that the Polish Army had rejected his orders to move against the seething cities. Also, Gomulka and his supporters had vowed to ask the people to fight if forced to. Khrushchev either had to put Russian soldiers in the field against Polish troops, or retreat. He chose to retreat.

In Hungary, matters proceeded differently. Here, too, there was deep political unrest. Workers, intellectuals, students, even army officers were caught up in the whirlpool of political dissatisfaction.

Matters became so bad that Khrushchev dispatched Mikoyan to Hungary. At a Central Committee meeting Matyas Rakosi, the Premier, was replaced by a man equally despised by his people, Erno Gero. The angry people held a mass meeting in Budapest in Parliament Square, thousands of them shouting for their hero, Imre Nagy. When a student delegation tried to force its way into the Radio Building in order to broadcast its message for reform, the political police used their guns.

Regular police and army units were summoned to help suppress the students and intellectuals. Instead the police and army

Bulganin (left) and Khrushchev are greeted in Czechoslovakia in 1957.

joined the rebels, turning their weapons over to the freedom fighters. Soon hundreds of trucks arrived carrying factory workers anxious to help. Hungary was caught up in a full-scale revolt.

Outside Budapest, the Red Army, in all its armored might, stood poised, waiting for orders. Khrushchev had learned a lesson in Poland and didn't intend to endure another setback here; he ordered the rebellion put down.

Soviet tanks rolled into Budapest. The fighting was fierce as more Hungarian soldiers joined the battle against the Russians. In the end, rifles had scant effect on armored cars and homemade Molotov cocktails could do only limited damage to Soviet tanks. With naked ferocity, the Red Army crushed the revolt.

On November 4, 1956, Radio Budapest broadcast its final plea for assistance. The freedom fighters cried out, but not to politicians or governments, aware that no help would come from those directions:

> This is the Hungarian Writers' Union. We are speaking to all writers, scientists, writers' and scientists' associations of the world, and to the intellectual leaders of all countries. Our time is limited. You know all the facts. No need to expand them. Long live Hungary. Help the Hungarian writers, scientists, workers, peasants and intelligentsia. Help! Help! Help!

No help came.

The world's attention focused on political-military adventures elsewhere. In the Middle East, President Gamal Abdel Nasser of Egypt nationalized the Suez Canal. In retaliation, England, France and Israel attacked that country.

The Israelis swept across the Sinai Desert with ease, but the English-French forces ran into difficulty. Anxious to prevent the seemingly inevitable defeat of Nassar, Khrushchev castigated the three warring nations, threatening to send rockets against English and French cities.

This drew a response from President Eisenhower indicating that such an attack might bring American rockets down on Russian cities. At the same time, Eisenhower, and his Secretary of State John Foster Dulles, exerted great pressure on England, France and Israel, demanding that they end their offensive.

The attackers were not able to withstand such pressure and the fighting ended. Though Egypt had been easily defeated by Israel, Nasser was still in power and he counted among his friends, Nikita Khrushchev. Russia had achieved a handhold in the Mediterranean, something the Czars had craved for two centuries.

Khrushchev, in typical fashion, had taken certain risks, the result being some gains and some losses. His manner of crushing the Hungarian revolt had cost him dearly among Communists outside the Iron Curtain. But he had fortified Russian influence and power in the Middle East. Overall, he was a winner and soon other events would crowd the brutality of Budapest into the shadows and he would appear to be a humanist dedicated to making a lasting world peace.

Yet, at the 1956-57 New Year's Eve party in the Kremlin, he voiced one of his famous toasts, declaring in dogmatic tones: "When it comes to the struggle against imperialism we are all good Stalinists."

He was saying, in effect, that for all the changes, very little had changed.

During his rise, Khrushchev had made a number of enemies. Some of them joined in an effort to unseat him as First Secretary, maneuvering and manipulating behind the scenes, and gathering strength where it most mattered, in the Presidium. They worked shrewdly and effectively and, when that body convened on June 21, 1957, they moved.

Despite a counter-attack by Khrushchev, a vote was taken and he was evicted from his job as First Secretary. This was a stunning blow, and it must have appeared to his enemies that they had finished him off, terminated his career. As a sop, they offered him the Ministry of Agriculture.

Khrushchev refused to succumb, refused to accept the will of the Presidium.

Bulganin, weak and acting as Premier only because of Khrushchev's indulgence, complained of his master's recalcitrance. "Well," he said, naively assuming that majority rule would inhibit a man of Khrushchev's indomitable spirit, "we are seven and you are four."

The round, peasant face flushed and the tiny eyes squinted. "In mathematics," he bit off, "two and two are indeed four, but that does not apply to politics."

He proceeded to tell his "equals" that they were not empowered to depose him, that only the Central Committee could do so. He insisted on a plenary session. Here was an unprecedented step, and none of them knew what to do.

Khrushchev acted promptly, causing hundreds of members of the Central Committee to be brought to Moscow—men who had long been his supporters, men deep in his debt for past favors, men who owed their careers to him and some who owed him their lives.

On June 23, the full session of the Committee met and the old Bolsheviks demanded Khrushchev's removal, accusing him of unsavory behavior by creating a cult of personality around himself and of making demagogic speeches in violation of Party doctrine.

They should have known better. To underestimate any enemy was fraught with danger; to underestimate Khrushchev could be lethal.

Marshal Zhukov, a hero of the struggle against the Nazis, rose to defend the First Secretary. There were others who were equally passionate, equally committed. A vote was called for which was carried by the friends of Nikita Khrushchev. Thus did he reap the rewards due for carefully tending to political details during his career.

Now it was Khrushchev's turn. He directed all his power and influence against the anti-Party group. Molotov, Malenkov, Kaganovich and their followers all were brutalized and thrown out of their high jobs. Reluctant, however, to publicly expose the degree of opposition he had faced, he kept Bulganin on as Premier and many others were not removed until after considerable time had elapsed.

In October, Khrushchev broke Marshal Zhukov, about whom he claimed, that a cult of personality had sprung up. The Marshal insisted on defying Party authority over the army, Khrushchev said. The First Secretary wanted no heroes on white horses raising enthusiastic public followings.

That same month, Russia launched the first man-made satellite around the earth—Sputnik. This triumph reflected favorably on Khrushchev and enhanced his standing both in Russia and around the world.

By March, 1959, he was ready to take a huge forward step. The delegates to the Supreme Soviet, gathered in the Great Hall of the Kremlin, showed no surprise when Premier Bulganin extended his resignation. But they were surprised when the chairman, Kliment Voroshilov, accepted it. They straightened up in their seats as Voroshilov rose to speak.

"Upon instruction by the Central Committee of the Communist Party of the Soviet Union," he said, "I propose to name Comrade Nikita Sergeyevich Khrushchev Chairman of the Council of Ministers and to charge him with forming a cabinet and submitting it to the Supreme Soviet . . . in addition to becoming Premier of the Soviet Union, Khrushchev should retain his position as First Secretary . . ."

Amidst sustained and stormy applause, the nomination was approved by acclamation. Khrushchev heaved himself erect, the peasant of Kalinovka standing with the tombs of the Czars under his feet, surrounded by all the pomp and circumstance of the Kremlin, accepting the homage of his associates, the first citizen of his country.

14

Chairman Khrushchev set his mind to two purposes: to better life in the Soviet Union and, in order to facilitate that process, to maintain world peace. To this end, he was convinced he had to meet with Western heads of state, specifically with the President of the United States, Dwight D. Eisenhower, and work out some kind of an accord.

Because he was deeply distrustful of the establishment in America, Khrushchev was certain that peace could come only out of meetings at the highest echelons. He wanted to convince Western leaders that he did not intend to use nuclear force to gain Soviet ends and wanted a similar assurance from them.

The history of the Communist Revolution, the imperialistic practices of many Western nations, the enmity of the United States through the years and her immense military and economic power, all served to create suspicion in Khrushchev's mind, and in the minds of people behind the Iron Curtain. When asked whether he truly believed the United States and her allies were readying themselves for aggressive acts against the USSR, he replied:

I consider that to be an indisputable fact . . . There is no doubt that the American people do not want war, but the United States of America is a highly developed centralized capitalist state, the Government of which represents big banks and monopolies . . . irresponsible people who for the sake of egoistic aims pursue an adventurist policy . . . the American people have practically no influence on the policies of the USA. They are cleverly tricked during election campaigns and virtually do not even know for what they are voting.

Despite these deep-rooted doubts, when he was invited, Khrushchev was eager to go to the United States, to meet with the President and create a relationship that might make possible peaceful coexistence. He also wanted to move past the barriers of diplomats and politicians and reach out to the ordinary people of America. He wished to let them get to know him, to learn about them, so as to convince them that it was possible for them to live in peace with his own people.

On September 14, 1959, the world was electrified by an announcement from Moscow. Soviet scientists had landed a rocket on the moon, the first time it had been done, an outstanding accomplishment that set Western military strategists to pondering. Obviously, the Soviet Union possessed rocketry systems capable of propelling a heavy work load over great distances with amazing accuracy. Their progress in fuel and telemetry systems was more advanced than that of the West.

On the next day, as if in counterpoint to that dramatic event, a huge TU 114 airliner settled down on the landing strip of Andrews Air Force Base outside Washington, D.C. American officials, led by President Eisenhower, waited to greet its exalted passenger, Nikita Sergeyevich Khrushchev. They were a somber group for they remembered Khrushchev's boastful threat to America—"We shall bury you."

The short, thick man who stepped off the plane was the same man who had warned Americans that their grandchildren would surely live under Communist rule, yet he was different. Instead of a sack suit that didn't fit, he wore a fashionable worsted suit, black Italian shoes, a white silk tie and gold cuff-links, and he carried a hat in his big hand.

He stood bareheaded under the hot sun while the President

delivered a short welcoming speech and he responded with a few words of his own. His reference to the Soviet moon shot brought dismay to his listeners at his lack of diplomacy. But some of them remembered that months before he had warned: "If other countries fight among themselves, they can be separated; but if war breaks out between America and our country, no one will be able to stop it. It will be a catastrophe on a colossal scale."

Before long, Khrushchev recognized that he was laboring under a severe handicap in America. His earlier declarations about overtaking the United States in all things and of turning her into a Communist state, all his threats were remembered and held against him. To most Americans he was inscrutable and ominous, the symbol of Soviet hostility and aggressiveness.

Unfortunately, ordinary men and diplomats alike overestimated his freedom to act independently. This was not another Stalin, not a total dictator. He was, instead, subjected to a variety of pressures at home from the Presidium, a restless population and the Red Army.

He had, in fact, become a victim of his own boasts, at home and abroad. To fulfill his promises to the Russian people, for example, the Soviet Union would be forced to utilize every resource, human and material. A crisis of any kind would strain those resources and force a rise in military budgets at the expense of industrial and agricultural development. Khrushchev knew that Russians were weary of war, wanted peace and prosperity and yearned to enjoy the product of their labors. Khrushchev hoped that this American visit would permit him to restructure the Soviet military establishment so as to achieve maximum security at minimum cost.

Not all Communists saw his desire for a *détente* with the West as a good thing. Mao Tse-tung, and his band of passionate revolutionaries in China, viewed violent conflict as the only solution to the struggle between capitalism and Communism.

148

This, and other differences, gave birth to a growing split in the Communist camp that some Western diplomats failed to recognize and understand, insisting that world Communism was monolithic in nature.

On the day after his arrival in Washington, a luncheon was held for Khrushchev at the National Press Club. He made a speech and questions were invited from the floor. A newsman wanted to know why Khrushchev had never spoken out against Stalin's excesses while the dictator lived.

When the question was translated into Russian, Khrushchev grew flushed and angry. Folds of livid skin seemed to encase his tiny eyes and his thorny hands formed into fists. An enraged outburst followed, an outpouring of peasant vituperation. Only the quick mind of the interpreter, softening his words, saved the moment from becoming a total disaster.

Again in Los Angeles, his ire was raised because he had been prevented, for security reasons, from visiting Disneyland. Here the Mayor persisted in questioning his "We shall bury you" remark. Khrushchev had earlier tried to explain that he had not meant those words literally, that it was a figure of speech not uncommon in the Russian vernacular. This continuous stress on what he considered unimportant and best forgotten served only to anger him again.

You know that I have come here with good intentions, but it appears that some of you would like to reduce matters to a joke. I repeat that it is a question of extremely serious things—a question of peace and war, of the life and death of people. We offer you the hand of friendship. If you don't want it, say so . . . Make your choice: shall we advance together to peace, or shall we continue the "cold war" and the arms race? I have not come to plead with you. We are no less strong than you. I have already made many speeches in the United States but have not once re-

sorted to the word "arms," let alone "missile." And if I
have spoken about it today, you must understand that I had
no choice.

At a subsequent meeting with a group of the country's foremost union leaders, Khrushchev became embroiled in a wild
political argument. Yet the next day he was in fine form, joking
and in high spirits, while talking with businessmen at the
California plant of International Business Machines.

"When I meet businessmen," he told these representatives of
the capitalistic system, "we find a common language in our
conversations. Being men of action we are quick to understand
one another."

During the tour, the Senate Foreign Relations Committee held
a reception for Khrushchev. The Senate Majority Leader, Lyn-
don B. Johnson, introduced the Chairman to a tall, slender
young Senator, John F. Kennedy.

"I have heard," Khrushchev said, "that despite your youth
you have a big future ahead of you."

Senator Kennedy acknowledged the compliment with a smile
and the two men shook hands. Destiny would bring them together again.

The high point of the trip was the two days spent in con-
versation with President Eisenhower at Camp David, Maryland.
In return for Eisenhower's agreement to explore the question
of a divided Germany, Khrushchev stated that he would not
press the issue of control over Berlin.

Khrushchev came away convinced he had persuaded Eisenhower that a great power summit meeting was desirable. It
also was agreed that the President's planned visit to Russia
should be postponed until the following spring in order that
his grandchildren might come along. It was a fateful decision.

Though nothing more concrete came out of those two days,
Khrushchev came to accept Eisenhower's sincere desire for

Dancers from the motion picture "Can-Can" chat with Khrushchev during his visit to California in 1959.

peace. But he gave him little credit otherwise, saying years later in a television interview:

> . . . People who knew Eisenhower as a military leader and a statesman . . . did not hold him in much respect either in one field or in the other. They considered him a mediocre general and a weak president, because of the softness of his character and one must admit that he is a good man. He easily fell under the influence of his aides and his subordinates . . . at every question . . . (he would) . . . immediately turn to his advisers and aides demanding explanations or answers to my questions . . .

To Khrushchev, who came to every meeting thoroughly prepared, and never would consider asking advice from a subordinate in public, this was unusual and unimpressive behavior.

"Such a President," Khrushchev said another time, "can take God knows what kind of decisions, and his is a vast, great and powerful nation. One shuddered at the thought that such great force was in such hands."

Such opinions may have been contributing factors in Khrushchev's behavior at a subsequent meeting between the two men.

Taking note of what had been said at Camp David, stressing the relaxed tensions between Russia and the United States and urging every nation to follow Soviet leadership, Khrushchev announced in January, 1960, that the Russian military would be cut by 1,200,000 men over the following eighteen months. He insisted that this made the Soviet Union the first power to cut its armed forces to the level suggested back in 1956 and asked the capitalist world to follow suit. He conveniently ignored the fact that both American and British military might were already at that level.

After a meeting with French President Charles de Gaulle in Paris, Khrushchev decided he would be unable to win a great diplomatic victory at a summit meeting. This troubled him, for he felt the need of some kind of dramatic triumph.

Domestic difficulties continued to plague him. A harvest failed in Kazakhstan. Dust storms were created by the eroded virgin lands, *his* virgin lands. There were economic slowdowns, due to industrial reforms instituted by him, and unrest among the generals displeased with the proposed cuts in military spending.

To make matters worse, there were those in the Communist orbit—in Russia, China, Czechoslovakia, East Germany—who heaped ridicule on Khrushchev's soft diplomacy, demanding a return to a hard foreign policy. Harassed, and anxious to protect his flanks from attack, Khrushchev issued a warning. If the West insisted on keeping soldiers in Berlin ". . . force will be opposed by force," and more, "Some people apparently hope to reduce . . . [the upcoming summit meeting] . . . to an ineffectual exchange of opinion . . . to evade concrete decisions. Such methods are least of all suited for dealing with the Soviet Union."

Here was Khrushchev, launching a war of nerves designed to confuse and confound, to intimidate. Threats of annihiliation were countered by vows of peace. Then, two weeks before the world leaders were due in Paris for the summit meeting, an event took place that changed everything.

Khrushchev was asleep when an American airplane flew high across the Soviet border, heading into the country. An aide woke the Chairman and told him that this was one of the U-2 planes used by the United States for scouting missions. Khrushchev accepted the news calmly and issued orders to keep him informed if there were further developments.

Khrushchev was not alarmed. He knew all about the U-2 overflights, designed to gather information, and that they had been going on since 1956. Up to now the Russians could do nothing about them and so made no complaints, anxious to conceal the fact that they lacked the military technology necessary to bring down the high-flying planes.

That had changed, however. Russian scientists had developed rockets capable of reaching to those heights where the U-2's flew.

Khrushchev was reviewing the traditional May Day parade in Red Square when he received word that the U-2 had been downed.

It was not until May 5, however, that Khrushchev announced that the spy plane had been shot down, giving no details at the time. Considering the circumstances, that his nation's sovereignty had been breached by the military aircraft of another country, he displayed a good deal of restraint. Part of this control stemmed from his desire to put an end to such flights by verbal pyrotechnics instead of with missiles and fighter planes.

As if determined to make a bad situation worse, the United States issued a "cover story" claiming that the plane had been on a meteorological mission, a weather plane. What authorities in Washington didn't know, was that the plane had not disintegrated upon being hit, as it was designed to do, and so its equipment and its pilot, Gary Francis Powers, had been captured.

That was precisely what Khrushchev had been waiting for. He pounced on the explanation of the United States, deriding it and naming the flight for what it truly was. He heaped scorn on the pilot's equipment—two gold watches, seven gold rings— "Perhaps," the Chairman said mockingly to the Supreme Soviet, "the pilot should have flown higher—to Mars, and was preparing to seduce Martian women?" French gold francs were found on Powers ". . . Nicely wrapped in cellophane in the American style."

At the same time, Khrushchev insisted that President Eisenhower could have known nothing about such flights. Here was Khrushchev the diplomat, offering his opposite number a way out of an embarrassing situation, anxious to gain a bargaining advantage, but careful not to disturb the peaceful nature of things between the two countries.

The United States State Department responded by admitting that spy planes had encroached on Soviet air space, but insisted that the Powers' flight had not been authorized in Washington.

Two days later Secretary of State Christian Herter stated that intelligence flights would continue and went so far as to suggest that the President himself had authorized them.

Khrushchev was furious. His magnanimous gesture had been rejected, embarrassing him before the world and before those of his own people who were less than enthusiastic with the way he was handling the situation. In anger, he talked loudly of Russian military capabilities, of rockets and the ease with which they could destroy the bases from which the U-2 planes took off. It was announced that Pilot Powers would be tried.

In defense of the U-2 campaign, President Eisenhower maintained that intelligence operations were vital to the well-being of the Western world.

Khrushchev responded in Moscow. The wreckage of the spy plane was displayed to the press. Spying could carry the nations of the world past the brink, he made clear, and to nuclear destruction. The American President, he went on bluntly, was no longer welcome in Moscow and he implied that this incident might very well have ended any real use for the Paris summit meeting.

"I am going to Paris on Saturday," he said, "but if some people want to prevent a conference, we can do without it. The Soviet Union has existed for forty years without a summit, and it can exist for one hundred more."

On May 14, Khrushchev arrived in Paris and informed President de Gaulle that he expected an apology from the United States. Two days later, he issued a blustering ultimatum:

The U.S. Government must firmly condemn . . . refrain from continuing such actions . . . against the U.S.S.R. . . .

155

It goes without saying that . . . the U.S. Government cannot fail to call to strict account those who are directly guilty of the deliberate violation by American aircraft of the borders of the U.S.S.R. Until this is done, the Soviet Government sees no possibility for productive negotiations with the U.S. Government at the summit conference . . .

He made no mention of Soviet espionage in the United States and elsewhere, even during those years when the two countries were joined in the struggle against Germany.

In response to the demand for an apology, President Eisenhower pointed out that ". . . In point of fact, these flights were suspended after the recent incident and are not to be resumed. Accordingly, this cannot be an issue."

But it was. In answer to suggestions that he should accept the Eisenhower statement, Khrushchev said, "That's a lackey's way. When a gentleman slaps a lackey's face and then gives him a sixpence, the lackey at once says thank you . . . But we know who we are and whom we represent."

The admissions by the State Department and by the President that the overflights had been authorized had caused public humiliation for Khrushchev and had supplied his domestic enemies with ammunition to use against him. By presenting an unyielding demeanor to the world, by publicly tongue-lashing the American President, by destroying the Paris summit with his tough, blunt language, Khrushchev was showing his associates in the Presidium, his "equals," that he was not weak toward capitalism.

15

For Khrushchev and for Russia, China was an immediate danger. Conflict between them was inevitable. Though both countries insisted that their futures were rooted in Marxist-Leninist principles, there were basic and abrasive differences that pushed them further and further apart.

The Soviet Union was a twentieth century nation in fact and in aspirations, becoming richer by Western standards, and anxious to benefit from the advantages of the contemporary world. China was not. In many ways, it still was shackled to ancient and outdated ways; its people were poor and backward. But China's leaders burned with revolutionary zeal and ruled a seething population that numbered in the hundreds of millions. The two countries also had a historical enmity that had caused frequent violent outbreaks along the extended Manchurian-Siberian frontier. The ingredients for increasing trouble were present.

Where Russia, under Khrushchev, was committed to peaceful coexistence with capitalism, China raised a loud voice in favor of violent revolution. The Chinese view was that the United States would seek to defend a weakening imperialistic position by launching local wars, and Peking wanted to provoke and support what it called wars of liberation, as was the case in Vietnam.

Behind the usual Communist screen of secrecy, high officials in Moscow began to fret about China's belligerence. Khrushchev was very concerned with the betterment of his people and, to this end, was committed to a system of material incentives, without which he was convinced an economy must fail. He ridiculed the Chinese, saying in 1962, "One must not imagine communism in the shape of a table at which are sitting 'highly politically conscious' and 'completely equal' people."

Sensitive to the widening of the breach between Mao Tse-tung and himself, Khrushchev tried to veil his position, attacking China only by indirection, by hitting out at Peking's staunch supporter in Europe, Albania. In 1960, he embarked on another Asian voyage and again tried to bring the message of Russia's increasing material wealth to the people of that region.

"Everywhere I speak with my own voice," he said in Calcutta, "expound my own convictions. But that doesn't oblige those to whom I speak to agree with my convictions. I say—this is what we have achieved in forty years of Soviet power. I say—this is what we were and what we have become . . . I do not boast. Figuratively speaking—the goods are their own recommendation."

This had no visible effect on the rulers of China, who continued to criticize the dictatorial methods of the Soviet Communist Party and to charge that the Kremlin had abandoned world revolution in favor of material security. Peaceful coexistence came in for a fair share of Chinese invective, which encouraged those back in Russia who felt likewise, and Khrushchev became aware of rising internal opposition.

As if responding to that irritant, he appeared at the United Nations session in New York City and promptly created a dramatic rumpus that drew world-wide attention to him. Annoyed that matters were not going his way, he took off his shoe and pounded it on the desk to indicate his displeasure. In the West, diplomats were startled and many people were amused at this colorful behavior; but in Moscow, importantly-placed men were dismayed and felt that such displays shamed the Soviet Union before the world, and their attitudes toward Nikita Sergeyevich grew harder.

In November, at a secret Moscow conference, the Chinese representative accused Khrushchev of betraying the Revolution and announced that Peking intended to assume leadership of the Communist movement. That same month, John Fitzgerald Kennedy, at age forty-three, was elected President of the United States.

Here was a fresh and comparatively unknown element on the world scene and Khrushchev was determined to test him, to take his measure. He remembered his one brief, uneventful meeting with the slender, young Senator who had been charming. Now they would meet again at a summit meeting in Vienna, as leaders of the world's two greatest powers.

Kennedy was the son of a rich father, a typical product of capitalism to Khrushchev, and that meant flawed, weak and having no real experience in the affairs of nations. Khrushchev saw him as a young man who had made no particular impression during his term in the Senate and who was barely a winner over Richard M. Nixon in the recent election. The international arena, it seemed to Khrushchev, was hardly the place for such a man to learn his job. But, if that was the way the United States functioned, the Chairman meant to take every advantage.

Still, when they met, Khrushchev displayed a cordial face to the young President. He told Kennedy that he still did not believe that Eisenhower had known about the U-2, and that he had accepted the blame only "in a spirit of chivalry." He also invited the President to visit Moscow. Though bursting with good will and lofty intentions, he made it clear that the USSR intended to give aid and comfort to revolutionary movements, wherever they existed. As for a nuclear test-ban, he was opposed to any such agreement. Russian science still wanted to conduct additional experiments, he said.

Later, Khrushchev would test President Kennedy in a more dramatic way. Many citizens of East Germany, disenchanted with life under Communist rule, were fleeing to freedom in West Germany. The German Communist regime was unhappy about this and decided to build a wall around that workers' paradise in order to keep the people from running away. Khrushchev gave support to the plan and the wall was erected. When the United States did nothing to stop it from going up and did not tear it down, Khrushchev felt certain that he understood and could deal easily with the new American President.

There was more to support that view. In Cuba, Fidel Castro had led a rebellion against the long-time dictator, Batista, and overthrown him. Entrenched in power, Castro now declared that his was a Communist Government. Many Cubans fled that island nation only ninety miles from Florida and took up residence in the United States where schemes were made to return to their homeland and to overthrow Castro.

On the night of April 16, 1961, twelve hundred Cuban exiles, armed and trained by the United States' Central Intelligence Agency (CIA), went ashore at the Bay of Pigs in an effort to reclaim the country from Castro. They failed. Political considerations and indecision insured the failure of the invasion. The Cuban patriots were defeated. To Khrushchev, who had put down the revolt of the Hungarian freedom fighters with ruthless efficiency, here was another sign of personal weakness in President Kennedy. This quality could be exploited for Khrushchev's gain.

Meanwhile, the quarrel between the Soviet Union and China grew more intense, the exchanges shriller, the insults more pointed, and there was an inevitable softening of Moscow's authority over the satellite countries.

Russia had severe domestic problems too. Industrial advances were slight; consumer items were hard to come by and of a poor quality. Farming quotas went unfulfilled. There was corruption and speculation, and central planning was ignored by many citizens. Russian youth, restless and arrogant, paid a minimum amount of respect to the Government and even less to the Party. Nor were they alone. Poets, writers and intellectuals openly criticized political leaders, past and present. The

Red Army's leaders were displeased with a diminished budget and fewer men in uniform, while emphasis was placed on missiles and nuclear arms.

Buffeted on all sides, Khrushchev cast about for some method of refurbishing Russia's image as the leader of the Communist movement and of polishing his diminished personal luster. Cuba seemed to offer the best chance.

A thorn in the tender side of the United States, Castro's island seemed ripe for a successful American invasion. Khrushchev meant to prevent that from happening. He came up with a daring move, one designed to reestablish his faltering prestige in one stroke. Here, in full view of the world, he would confront the young American President and deal him a stunning defeat. He would show everyone how well the Soviet Union could protect Communist nations, no matter where they were located, and, at the same time, deliver a telling military blow to the West.

If he needed further justification for what he had planned, Khrushchev found it in President Kennedy's own words regarding Cuba: "We shall continue to work with Cuban refugee leaders who are dedicated as we are to that nation's future return to freedom. We shall continue to keep the American people and the Congress fully informed. We shall increase our surveillance of the whole Caribbean area."

There was the United States' declared intention to launch another invasion of Cuba. Khrushchev moved. With support from some of his colleagues, and surely from his generals, he ordered the swift and secret installation of intermediate range missiles in Cuba, rockets armed with nuclear warheads, all aimed at vulnerable locations on the American mainland. Once placed, those missiles would protect Cuba from invasion for surely, no American President would dare a nuclear war for the sake of that island nation. And Khrushchev would have what he needed —a military advantage and a propaganda victory.

Once the decision was made, no time was wasted. By the end

of July, Russian ships loaded with nuclear bombs, rockets and guidance systems were at sea, steaming toward Cuba. Technicians and military advisers were flown in and work began. To disguise all this activity, Khrushchev announced that he was going to provide material and personnel to help Cuba construct a fishing port, insisting that Russia had no need of a military base on the island.

For Fidel Castro, this was a guarantee of his continued political existence, though he undoubtedly misunderstood Khrushchev's intentions. The Russian strong man never intended for the "volatile" Cubans to control the rockets.

But, for all their planning, Khrushchev and Castro both failed to reckon with the highly developed surveillance techniques carried on by the American military. Planes, equipped with the most recent photographic developments, penetrated the most sophisticated concealment efforts. Experts at translating aerial photographs were able to report what was happening in Cuba.

On October 19, President Kennedy, who was travelling the United States in a Congressional election campaign, broke off his speech-making and returned to Washington. It was said that a bad cold had caused his change of plans.

The President had hoped to withhold news of the fast-developing crisis until he and his advisers had decided how to handle it. But the story broke prematurely, and there was considerable agitation for a swift military strike against Cuba. Determined not to be bullied into a rash act, an act that might plunge the world into the horror of nuclear war, the President discussed every possibility with the men around him.

Finally, unable to remain silent any longer, President Kennedy went before the American people to tell them that the Soviet Union was erecting missile sites in Cuba and that these sites were a direct danger to American security. He demanded their immediate removal, vowing to bend every effort to that end, while trying to maintain peace.

Khrushchev attends a United Nations session in 1960 with A. A. Gromyko (left), then Minister for Foreign Affairs.

At the same time, the military was mustered to fighting readiness. The Navy stood at sea and the Air Force was alerted. The Army sent combat-ready troops into Florida and other points of departure. Long-range missiles were made ready in their silos, the Strategic Air Command sent its huge bombers aloft and Polaris submarines, each with sixteen nuclear missiles, plowed to strategic points under the seas.

· Messages between Washington and Moscow were exchanged. This time President Kennedy's grasp of the situation and his ability to deal with a crisis situation without losing his nerve, swung the balance of power in his direction. He was informed that none of the launching pads had been completed which meant that Khrushchev had allowed himself to be placed in an impossible position. He had hoped to squeeze the President into a corner; instead, he found himself trapped.

· He had assumed he could make Kennedy back down, certain the President would not risk nuclear war over Cuba. Now the President was in a position to make that same assumption about him. To stand against America's demand for withdrawal would invite further action and put Khrushchev in the position of being the aggressor.

Having begun this dangerous adventure, he intended to follow it through as far as possible and so he placed the Red Army on a readiness basis, but he was careful not to create a crisis atmosphere in Russia. Anxious to show no undue alarm, he gave an interview to an American businessman, appeared in public in his usual way and talked with an American opera singer at the Bolshoi Theatre. He was determined that there would be no nuclear war but he wanted to be certain that he could not obtain his goal without conflict before he would back off.

· Once convinced that President Kennedy and the United States would fight if pushed too hard, he acted in a rational manner. He ordered Russian ships, then heading for Cuba with more equipment, to turn back, avoiding contact with American naval vessels standing in their path.

Still he tried to bargain. He wrote to the President on October 26, saying he would remove his missiles if Kennedy would guarantee there would be no invasion of Cuba. The next day he demanded publicly that the United States remove its rockets from bases in Turkey. He was trying to win whatever was possible from the situation, and not give in too readily.

In the end, Khrushchev was forced to come to grips with the reality of this ominous charade. He had underestimated President Kennedy and the resolve of the American people. Left at last with only one choice, he took his rockets away from Fidel Castro and Cuba.

Years later, in a television interview, Khrushchev recalled that tense time and offered his interpretation of what had happened.

Perhaps we shouldn't have done it, but, if the rockets had not been installed, would there be a Cuba now? No, it would have been wiped out. And if that is true, it means that our transportation of rockets was justified. It cost us money but we did not lose a single man. We took our rockets and bombers away in exchange for President Kennedy's promise not to invade Cuba . . . He gave us his promise to carry his part and we carried out ours. And that's the way we liquidated the possibility of beginning a nuclear war.

Impressed with President Kennedy as a worthy opponent, one he could deal with and trust, Khrushchev continued to work for a greater understanding with the United States.

When he signed a nuclear test-ban treaty with the West, much of the world experienced a sense of relief. But not China. Peking raged at Khrushchev and declared that Russia had refused to help China develop its own nuclear force, thus abrogating a mutual technical assistance pact agreed to in 1957.

In 1962, as part of his program to enhance the quality of

165

existence in the Soviet Union, Khrushchev defended a number of works of art which were anti-Stalin in theme. He had even permitted publication of the novel, *One Day in the Life of Ivan Denisovich,* which exposed the labor camps of Siberia and previously had been suppressed. When his liberalism was opposed, especially by the Party's foremost ideologist, Mikhail Suslov, Khrushchev struck back by using his opponents' own weapons.

At a meeting of Russia's leading writers and artists in the spring of 1963, he levelled criticisms at their liberal attitudes and at their emphasis on the abstract in their work, demanding more political orthodoxy. But there was a strong streak of independence in the young artists.

One of the most daring of them, Yevgeny Yevtushenko, a rising poet, had written about the thousands of Jews who had been murdered by German storm troopers outside of Kiev, with no one in the Ukraine coming to their assistance. In part, his poem said:

> Let the Internationale ring out,
> When the last anti-Semite on earth is buried.
> There is no Jewish blood in mine,
> But I am hated by every anti-Semite as a Jew,
> And because of this, I am a true Russian.

Yevtushenko was reminded that the Constitution of the USSR guaranteed equality to all people and was told no anti-Semitism existed in the country. The poet rejected this oversimplified explanation and insisted that anti-Semitism did exist and must be eliminated.

Khrushchev became enraged and leaped to his feet. "Stop it!" he cried. "Anti-Semitism is not a problem in the Soviet Union."

Yevtushenko refused to give way. "Yes, Nikita Sergeyevich, it is a problem."

"No problem!" Khrushchev bellowed. "No problem!"

The argument went on and when another artist was criticized for his work, Yevtushenko admitted the possibility of error, saying that any mistakes would surely be corrected.

"A hunchback will only be straightened in the grave," Khrushchev said coldly.

Yevtushenko showed no fear. "I believed that the time had passed when the grave was considered to be a method of straightening."

A wave of applause went up from the audience and, after a moment, Khrushchev had no choice but to join in. Moments later he was back on the attack. Peaceful coexistence was one thing, he made clear, but there was going to be no ideological tolerance of capitalism and Western ways. He insisted that there had to be political conformity from all Soviet citizens, even those who labored in cultural vineyards. All this would return to haunt Khrushchev in the near future.

But first, on November 22, 1963, came a shattering moment, for him personally, for the United States and for all the peoples of the world.

John Fitzgerald Kennedy, 35th President of the United States, was assassinated.

16

The world changed. Techniques which once had been effective now ran into difficulties; different conditions required new approaches; collective leadership created problems for a strong man with a natural inclination to wield power, unfettered by restrictions.

Perhaps more than any other single factor, the soft condition of Soviet economy provided ammunition for Khrushchev's enemies in the Kremlin.

In 1959, he predicted that Russia would exceed the United States in both gross and *per capita* income by 1970.

Two years later, he cried: "The present generation of Soviet people will live under Communism . . . We base ourselves on strictly scientific estimates, which indicate that we shall, in the main, have built a communist society within twenty years."

This Communism, this ideal condition, was ticked off in detail. By 1980, *per capita* income would have reached a point 250 times as great as that of 1960. Every family would live in its own apartment; public utilities would be provided at no cost; food would be in abundance. In these boasts, Khrushchev placed his reputation on the line, and he took on personal responsibility for agriculture.

All his predictions were wrong, and he lost standing with his associates. Industrial production fell from eleven per cent in 1959 to 7½ per cent in 1964; consumer goods dropped to a growth rate of only two per cent. The housing industry failed to meet the demands of the Seven Year Plan.

Leonid Brezhnev (left) presents Khrushchev with a gold star of Hero of the Soviet Union shortly before Khrushchev's fall from power.

Even in farming, Khrushchev's specialty, the annual rise was only 1.7 per cent, less than the yearly rise in population.

The generals also were unhappy. They pointed out that in 1961 the United States enlarged its military budget and insisted that Russia must do likewise. They got their way, and, soon thereafter, Russia resumed nuclear testing.

Khrushchev went before the Central Committee to demand that the production of farming machinery, a costly program, be doubled. His request was turned down, the most acute defeat he had suffered since becoming Premier.

Desperate for the money for agriculture, Khrushchev agreed to an increase in meat prices of thirty per cent and in butter of twenty-five per cent. There was considerable grumbling at all levels, and unfavorable comparisons were made with the Stalin-era when retail prices were often lowered each year.

A month before the Cuban missile crisis, Khrushchev had made another mistake. He told the Presidium that he intended to split the Party into two sections, industrial and agricultural. The plan was a blueprint for increased Party control over the economy. The Presidium approved, but only under the most intense pressure. Here was another indication of Khrushchev's inclination to act on his own and to ignore the collective leadership.

Members of the apparatus became alarmed at this tendency on his part to autocracy and adventurism, as the missile crisis had made evident.

Then he went further, announcing new ideas for increasing farm production and suggesting general use of chemical fertilizers, pesticides, herbicides and artificial foodstuffs. Once again, he was calling for what earlier he had been unable to win—investment in the chemical industry.

Soon it became apparent that his land program had turned in a different direction. Before, he had fought for an extension of the area under cultivation. Now he was trying instead to intensify farming methods.

But his program was in trouble, and all signs indicated that the upcoming harvest would be a poor one; it became necessary to ration flour and bread throughout the land.

Undeterred, Khrushchev developed a Five Year Plan, aimed at increasing the production of consumer goods and services. To many of his colleagues, this was just another attempt to downgrade heavy industry at the expense of the military. Many state officials, military men, bureaucrats and industrial managers voiced their opposition to these schemes.

There were other things that troubled them about Nikita Sergeyevich. There were his continuing battle with China and Mao Tse-tung, and his obvious attempt to impose his will in all matters, often without consulting anyone else. He used his son-in-law Alexei Adzhubei, editor of the Government newspaper *Izvestia,* in an attempt at personal diplomacy with West Germany. There were troublesome rumors abroad that he intended to raise Adzhubei, a man who was unqualified and unpopular inside the Soviet Union, to a high government job.

On September 30, 1964, Khrushchev, First Secretary of the Soviet Communist Party and Chairman of the Council of Ministers of the USSR, left Moscow for the Black Sea resort area of Gagra. He was weary and in need of a vacation, a change of scenery, a chance to replenish his energies. Upon his arrival, he was met by a limousine which carried him over the final eighteen miles to his villa at Cape Pitsunda. The villa was a splendid place to rest in seclusion, set deep in a state farm and surrounded by a piney woods. It had a heated pool in which Khrushchev liked to swim now and then.

The days passed quietly with only a few visitors. He had all the time he wanted in which to prepare his agricultural speech for a special session of the Central Committee.

One visitor was unexpected. Anastas Mikoyan came to attempt to persuade him to compromise with his opponents regarding his farming and financial reforms. But Khrushchev was stubborn, confident he was right, and would not be budged. He had been through too many intramural battles, and had won too many of them, to be fearful of those who might dare to stand opposed to his wishes.

Early on the morning of October 13, Khrushchev welcomed M. Gaston Palewsky, a French official. He ushered his visitor into his study and they spoke amiably for some time. Without warning, one of the Chairman's aides rushed in, speaking quietly, urgently. Khrushchev's little eyes narrowed, and he heaved himself erect. The meeting with the Frenchman was over.

It was a somber Khrushchev who was driven to the nearest airport, where he discovered that his private plane was absent. Another plane had been flown in from Moscow. His crew had orders to bring him back to the capital city.

At that moment, Khrushchev understood that the enemies he had scorned, mocked, ignored and bypassed in so many matters were finally striking back. Obviously they intended to remove from his powerful shoulders the mantle of power he had worn for so long.

He snorted, climbed into the plane and strapped himself into a seat. To defeat Nikita Sergeyevich was no easy thing and never had been, not even in his early days back in Kalinkova. His enemies dared to challenge him; they wanted a fight. He would give them more than they wanted.

17

It was an ordinary fall day in Moscow, with a suggestion of winter in the air. People hurried about their affairs, anxious to take advantage of the last of the good weather. Shoppers crowded into the stores and housewives searched for fresh food for that night's dinner. In Red Square, workers put up posters and other decorations for the rally which was to celebrate the flight of the spacecraft *Voskhod I,* a great triumph for Soviet technology. The *Voskhod's* three cosmonauts were to be received as heroes.

In Staraya Square, the atmosphere was less festive. Outside the somber Central Committee Building, a formation of black *Chaika* limousines was drawn up. An astute observer, knowing that the luxury cars were supplied only to top echelon officials, might have guessed that the Presidium was in session and had been for most of the morning.

None of the members of that high body held any doubts as to what had to be done. Only techniques concerned them now: how to achieve their ends most efficiently. They were all agreed: Nikita Sergeyevich Khrushchev had to be removed from all power.

That was easier said than done. The old peasant was a tough and wily fighter hardened over the years in the demanding arena of Communist Party battling and wise to all the tricks, many of which he had invented himself. Planning would have to be thorough, precise.

173

They recalled other attempts to oust him: each time he had skillfully eluded them, going directly to the Central Committee and its 330 members, appealing successfully for their support. His charismatic personality had always served him well, and his ability as an agitator still was sharp.

To arm themselves against possible counter-attack, certain delicate moves were in order. Steps were taken to isolate the First Secretary from the people, who perhaps were his major source of strength. This required keeping the avenues of communication, the newspapers, the radio and television, closed to him. The secret police network working within these media were brought to a condition of increased vigilance, so that Alexei Adzhubei and others would be unable to move if Khrushchev called for help.

As for the Central Committee, it counted many old and loyal Khrushchev men in its ranks. But the members of the Presidium were good students and had learned from the master himself. Back in 1957, when he had been under attack, he had flown his supporters into Moscow, at the same time neglecting to notify those whom he suspected might vote against him. Now the Presidium could and would do no less. Choosing carefully, they contrived a quorum from the roster of the Central Committee, conveniently omitting Khrushchev's friends.

At two o'clock that afternoon, Khrushchev arrived at Venukovo Airport. A car and a detachment of bodyguards were waiting. He knew no one; they were under the personal command of the chief of the Secret Police, Vladimir Semichastny. Khrushchev grunted knowingly. Here was a tableau which had confronted many other Soviet officials.

He ducked into the limousine. Already plotting his strategy against what he knew must lie ahead, he paid no attention as the big car tooled along Kutuzovsky Prospect, rolling across the Moscow River and into the New Arbat, past the Manege, the old riding school and, finally, through the Kremlin wall.

He went directly to his office and tried to telephone his sup-

A crowd gathers in Red Square to welcome the Voskhod astronauts, unaware that Khrushchev has been removed from office.

porters, but without success. All their telephone numbers had been changed during his stay at the Black Sea. He paid silent, grudging admiration to the thoroughness of his enemies and understood that no choice remained except to confront them directly. He picked his way unhurriedly through the ancient corridors to the room where the Presidium was waiting.

All heads swung in his direction when he entered. He stared at them coldly. Leonid Brezhnev, for so long his lieutenant, was seated in the chairman's chair, *Khrushchev's* chair. A single gesture indicated that the Premier was to sit alongside him.

Brezhnev waited until Khrushchev was settled. Then, in a confidential voice, he told him that the Presidium was willing to accept his resignation and to provide him with an honorable withdrawal from public life. A gracious public farewell would be welcomed, Khrushchev was informed, at which time he could nominate Brezhnev as his successor as First Secretary of the Party.

"No political leader should relinquish his power of his own free will," Khrushchev had once said. He made it clear that he still clung to that view. He would fight against the conspirators.

It was hopeless, he was warned. The Party, the Government, the Red Army and the Secret Police all were arraigned against him. His victory was impossible.

He shook his head. Nothing was impossible for Nikita Sergeyevich Khrushchev, a peasant boy of Kalinovka, a man who had worked the mines of the Donets Valley, a man who had survived the Great Purge and achieved the highest posts in the Soviet Union. He demanded his right to place his case before the Central Committee.

The Presidium agreed.

The next day, the delegates came together in the headquarters of the Central Committee. Amidst an air of mystery and tension, they wondered why they were there and why so many others were missing.

Though the proceedings were intended to remain secret, a

forty-page summary was later distributed to be read to Party members, so what took place became public knowledge.

It was the ideological authority, Mikhail Suslov, who presented the Presidium's case.

"This man," he said, pointing to Khrushchev, flushed and drawn tight on a bench across the room, "this man has become vain. This man has forgotten his conscience.

"The principle damage done by Comrade Khrushchev's personal initiatives, particularly after 1962, was in the disorganization of the Party and in his mismanagement of agricultural and industrial production."

Suslov specified Khrushchev's ideological sins. He had split the Party in two, one section for farming and another for industry, resulting in chaos. He had undermined the authority of the Central Committee. He had ". . . repeatedly transgressed and violated the principle of collective leadership . . ." developing his own cult of personality.

Here was the key charge—Khrushchev had tried to transform himself into a dictator and, in doing so, had spread confusion and ruin across the country.

It is in his agricultural policy that Comrade Khrushchev has most clearly demonstrated his failure to assess problems soberly . . . a campaign to abolish the practice of rotating crops and introduce the intensive cultivation of maize to provide animal fodder. This measure was, perhaps, a suitable one for some regions, but in others it resulted in serious crop failures and the further exhaustion of already infertile soil, as well as in a deplorable confusion in agricultural administration. Then, Khrushchev changed his mind and decided that the way to agricultural success lay in the rapid development of the fertilizer industry.

He cited the coddling of light industry at the expense of heavy machinery. As a result, he said, steel production fell off and iron ore mining was prevented from introducing modern techniques. Also, because of this, pipes large enough to bring oil from the Asian fields to the refineries had been impossible to manufacture. The military establishment continued to be frustrated by his opposition to their demands and his concentration on rocketry and nuclear arms.

More criticism came. Khrushchev was described as impulsive and dangerous to the Soviet Union. His personal behavior frequently had been unacceptable in a man of such high estate. The shoe-banging at the United Nations, public claims of secret weapons capable of destroying the world, boasts of egg production that were patently false, insulting attitudes directed toward diplomats at home and abroad, and the arrogant placement of his son-in-law, Adzhubei, his wife and his children in high jobs, were cited.

In foreign affairs, there were many failures to catalogue: military assistance sent to India during its frontier conflict with China, a Communist country; the worsening relations with China; the partial rupturing of relations with Rumania; the Cuban missile adventure which was viewed as a defeat for Russia.

"A change of leader has become necessary," Suslov said, ending his five-hour charge, "because of Comrade Khrushchev's excessively personal policies, and because he has refused to honor the principle of collective leadership."

Others spoke against Khrushchev. Their anger was aimed at his impulsiveness, his plans that went nowhere, his abrupt changes in policy, his opportunism and his boasts. He was blamed for the restlessness in the satellites and his own anxiety to come to an understanding with the United States. They said that the business of the Party and of the nation, were too involved and too important to be left in the hands of a man given to impulse and to sudden rages.

Withdraw, they insisted. Quit.

He never had learned how to quit, so he fought back.

He reminded them that it had been Khrushchev who had guided the USSR through a period of great change, into the atomic age, the age of missiles. When there had been trouble and others had vacillated and shown fear, he had been resolute, decisive, bold. In a world geared for sudden destruction, he had maintained peace. Where poverty had once been the way of life, he had brought food and work to the people.

He attacked his attackers in the only way he knew. His big fists pounded at the air and he forged ahead wildly and often without restraint, a performance that seemed to many of those in attendance to justify the charges. The Soviet Union enjoyed a wealth and security it had never experienced before. Khrushchev had made all of this happen. Could any among them have done as well?

None could deny his accomplishments, his drive, his ability, his natural intelligence or his courage. An era of transition lay behind them and a vital role had had to be played. Perhaps only he could have played it. But that was past, another time, and he was a prisoner of that time, with his usefulness used up. He was too old.

They listened to him and, when he was through, they voted.

On October 15, people waiting in Pushkin Square for the first edition of *Izvestia* were told that there would be no paper that night. They went home curious, but not too curious.

Later that evening, the huge portrait of Khrushchev, which decorated the tall Moskva Hotel across from the Kremlin, was taken down.

At midnight, the TASS international service wire began to click off a message. It reported:

Nikita Khrushchev has been released of the duties as the First Secretary of the CPSU Central Committee and chairman of the Council of Ministers of the U.S.S.R. Leonid

Brezhnev has been elected First Secretary of the CPSU Central Committee. Alexei Kosygin has been appointed chairman of the Council of Ministers.

It has been announced today that a plenary meeting of the CPSU Central Committee held on Wednesday, October 14, considered Khrushchev's request to be relieved of his duties "in view of his advanced age and deterioration of his health."

Nikita Sergeyevich left Moscow that night unnoticed, weary and defeated. For the first time in half-a-century, he was a private man, silent and alone.

18

Khrushchev was a complicated man, of many parts, and his time in power reflected this. In a nation where elections confirmed personalities and policies rather than electing popularly chosen officials, where a political party, *the* Party, had ultimate authority over the Government, where the leading newspaper, *Pravda,* was an organ of official opinion, he was the inevitable product of the system, its pride and its prisoner.

A man of obvious contradictions, he led the Soviet Union through a period of change. He perceived the need for change, recognized its inevitability, yet, like the country itself, was unable to fully accommodate himself to it. He encouraged writers and artists to greater freedom of expression, then hit out at them for ideas which were not in keeping with official thought.

Functioning within an authoritarian political framework, through which he had progressed, he could never entirely free himself of its disciplines. As the Party insisted on its right to dictate in all matters, so did the man who became its leader.

By ending the tyranny of Stalinism, he had insured his own downfall, alerting his colleagues to the dangers of another dictator.

A man of the people, Khrushchev was capable of imposing cruelties on the citizens of Russia. A pragmatic man, concerned with results, he was able to put aside all dogma and make alliances with men and with nations who had been his enemies.

Although he was able to grasp the essence of most situations

181

quickly, he had failed to understand that, with the easing of Stalinism's rigid controls over the Communist world, the satellites would demand more and more independence, the Kremlin's authority would diminish, and Russia's prestige would lessen.

He believed that nuclear weapons made peaceful coexistence with the West a necessity. But he remained convinced that, in time, Communism would destroy capitalism. To this end, he supported "wars of liberation," keeping pressure on the United States. Because of this duality, he never was able to achieve the stable working relationship with the West which he desired.

Paternalism and tyranny were the Cain and Abel of Khrushchev's reign, the forces in conflict. A tempestuous man, a blusterer, a gambler given to taking dangerous risks, he was also an idealist who believed in the future of his people, and now hoped for a peace that would secure that future. He had been able to go into an alien world he never fully understood, hoping to learn about its ways, hoping its people would understand him. He was the first Soviet leader to do this and appeared to enjoy the experience, which must have raised doubts about him among his more solemn and somber colleagues.

The brashness he exhibited, his crudeness, his pleasure at basking in the public spotlight, were the weaknesses which led to his downfall. They also were his strengths and contributed to the length of his political life. Most important, he was a man who got things done.

Seeking always to modify and change the world, he remained constant himself. Driven by personal pride, as well as national concern, he often acted in terms of his own career, his own public image. Impatient, and too often short-sighted, he failed to make needed reforms because he was unable to erect the foundation on which to build.

At this writing, he has been shunted aside. He lives in an imposing dacha only seventeen miles from the Kremlin, but light years away from any role in public events. He is a pen-

Khrushchev in retirement, 1967.

sioner of the state, receiving about six hundred dollars a month; his rent is paid.

He is interested in photography and spends much of his time taking pictures and developing them in his own darkroom. This is a far cry from the conflicts of the past, from the excitement of making great decisions, of confronting world leaders. But he can comfort himself in the knowledge that, when all is weighed and measured, it must be said that the Soviet Union has become a better place since he began to govern it.

He keeps a modest apartment in Moscow, a voting address, and when last he went to the polls with Nina Petrovna, hundreds of Soviet citizens surrounded him, smiling warmly.

"Pust budit mir," he told them. "Let there be peace."

Bibliography

Archer, Jules, *Man of Steel, Joseph Stalin.* New York, Julian Messner, 1965.

Barbusse, Henri, *Stalin.* New York, The MacMillan Company, 1935.

Crankshaw, Edward, *Khrushchev, A Career.* New York, The Viking Press, 1966.

Davies, Joseph E., *Mission To Moscow.* New York, Simon and Schuster, 1941.

Deutscher, Isaac, *The Unfinished Revolution (1917-1967).* London, Oxford U. Press, 1967.

Douglas, William O., *Russian Journey.* Garden City, N.Y., Doubleday & Co., Inc., 1956.

Dulles, Allen, *The Craft of Intelligence.* New York, Harper & Row, 1963.

Frankland, Mark, *Khrushchev.* New York, Stein and Day, 1967.

Hayter, Sir William, *The Kremlin and the Embassy.* New York, The MacMillan Co., 1967.

Heilbroner, Robert L., *The Worldly Philosophers.* New York, Simon and Schuster, 1953.

Katkov, George, *Russia 1917: The February Revolution.* New York, Harper & Row, 1967.

Kellen, Konrad, *Khrushchev, A Political Portrait.* New York, Frederick A. Praeger, Inc., 1961.

Kennen, George F., *Russia and the West.* Boston and Toronto, Little, Brown and Co., 1961.

Massie, Robert K., *Nicholas and Alexandra.* New York, Atheneum Publishers, 1967.

MacGregor-Hastie, Roy, *The Man From Nowhere*. New York, Coward-McCann, Inc., 1961.

Moorehead, Alan, *The Russian Revolution*. New York, Harper & Brothers, 1958.

Paloczi-Horvath, George, *Khrushchev*. Boston, Little, Brown and Co., 1960.

Page, Martin, *The Day Khrushchev Fell*. New York, Hawthorn Books, Inc., 1965.

Payne, Robert, *The Fortress*. New York, Simon and Schuster, 1967.

Taylor, A. J. P., *The Origins of the Second World War*. New York, Atheneum Publishers, 1961.

Thayer, Charles W., *Russia*. New York, Time, Inc., 1963.

Trotsky, Leon, *Stalin*. New York and London, Harper & Brothers, 1941.

Truman, Harry S., *1945: Year of Decisions*. Garden City, N.Y., Doubleday & Co., Inc., 1955.

Truman, Harry S., *1946-1952: Years of Trial and Hope*. Garden City, N.Y., Doubleday & Co., Inc., 1956.

Werth, Alexander, *Russia at War*. New York, E. P. Dutton & Co., 1964.

Index

Mensheviks, 9
Mikoyan, Anastas, 44, 88, 96, 114, 115, 128, 136, 171
Molotov, Vyacheslav Mikhailovich, 34, 47, 62, 76, 88, 91, 96, 106, 114, 136, 137, 139, 145
  Khrushchev's attack on 121, 122
Moscow, 36-37, 39, 48-49
Moscow Subway, 124
  building of, 49-56
  described, 56-57
Moyseenko, K. V., 27, 28

Nagy, Imre, 140
Nasser, Gamal Abdel, 142-143
New Economic Policy, 22
Nicholas II, Czar, 7, 8-9, 10, 11, 14
  abdication of, 15
  death of, 18
Nikolayev, Leonid, 61, 62
NKVD (People's Commissariat for Internal Affairs—Secret Police), 59, 60, 63, 75, 76

One Day in the Life of Ivan Denisovich, 166
Operation Barbarossa, 80
Ordzhonikidze, 44

Palewsky, M. Gaston, 172
Peasants, 7-8, 10-12, 20-21, 34, 38, 57
Petrograd, 9, 14, 15
Piatakov, 29
Poland, 19, 78-79, 139-140
Politburo, 34, 47, 71, 93, 119, 125
Pomerantisev, V., 110

Pospelov, 102
Postyshev, Pavel P., 72-73, 85, 131
Powers, Gary Francis, 154, 155
Pravda, 13, 29, 39, 40-42, 63
Presidium, 93, 102, 103, 137, 139, 143-144, 170
Proletarian Revolution, 45
Purge (Great Purge), 63, 66-67, 71, 72, 129

Rakosi, Matyas, 140
Red Army, 16, 25, 78, 79, 84, 105-106, 122, 142
Red Presnaya District, 43, 46
Red Terror, 17-18
Right Deviationists, 34, 38, 40-42
Rokossovsky, Marshal, 140
Romanov Dynasty, 7, 10, 13
Roosevelt, Franklin Delano, 57, 97
Rudzutak, 131
Rukhzade, 104
Russia
  agriculture in, 37-38, 91-92, 110-112, 170, 177
  anti-semitism in, 166-167
  changes in, after denunciation of Stalin, 138-139
  domestic problems, 160-161, 168-171
  famine in, 18-19, 46, 57
  liberal attitude of intellectuals, 110, 124, 166-167
  as nuclear power, 109, 170
  after revolution, 16
  space accomplishments, 145, 147, 173
Russian Revolution, 14-19, 134
Ryumin, 104

St. Petersburg, 9
Salinsky, A., 110
Secret police of Russia, 17, 27
    See also NKVD
Secretariat, 103
Semichastny, Vladimir, 174
Serov, Ivan Alexandrovich, 78, 79
Shatalin, 102
Shirin, A. P., 42, 43
Slutsky affair, 45-46
Social Democratic Party, 8, 9, 15
"Socialism in One Country," 26
Socialist Revolutionaries, 15, 17
Sokolnikov, 29
Sputnik, 145
Stalin, Joseph Dzhugashvili
    conflict with Bukharin, 33-35
    deification campaign, 64-66, 73, 86
    denunciation of, 128-137
    "de-Stalinization process," 138
    Great Purge of, 59-63, 66-67, 71, 72
    Khrushchev's relationship with, 90
    poem to, 85-86
    resignation of, 47
    rise to power, 28-29
    stroke and death of, 97-101
Stalingrad, 82
Stepanov, A. M., 51
Summit meeting (Geneva), 121-122
Suslov, Mikhail, 102, 128, 166, 177
Suvorov, 55

Timashuk, 95
Timoshenko, Semyon, 78
Tito, Marshal, 119, 120, 121, 126, 139

Tokuda, 127
Trotsky, Leon, 10, 15, 21, 26, 29, 59, 136
    death of, 70
    in exile, 62
    indictment against, 71
    quoted, on Communist Party, 25
Trotskyites, 45-46, 62, 66, 67, 68-70
Tyagnibeda, 55

Ukraine, 18, 73-74
    Khrushchev's work in, 72, 74-76, 78-80, 81, 84, 89, 90
Ukrainian nationalists, 28
United Nations, 158
United States, 57, 112-114, 137
    Khrushchev's fear of, 125, 146
    Khrushchev's visit to, 147-152
U-2 plane incident, 153-156, 159

Vassilevsky, Marshal, 94
Vatutin, 86
Vinogradov, Professor, 94, 95
Virgin Lands agricultural plan, 111-112, 114
Voroshilov, Kliment, 44, 46, 62, 88, 91, 96, 136, 137, 145

West Germany, 125
Witte, Count, 10
World War I, 13, 14, 17
World War II, 78-82, 125

Yagoda, Henry, 45, 59, 67
Yenukidze, A. S., 66
Yevtushenko, Yevgeny, 166-167
Yezhov, Nikolai Ivanovich, 44-45, 66-67, 75, 131

191

Yezhovchina, 67
Yugoslavia, 119-120
Yuzovka, 26

Zhdanov, Andrei, 88, 94

Zhukov, Marshal Grigori, 102, 121, 144, 145
Zinoviev, Grigori, 29, 59, 61-62, 64, 67
Zinovievites, 70